RUTH FIELDING IN MOVING PICTURES

OR, HELPING THE DORMITORY FUND

ALICE B. EMERSON

1st WORLD
LIBRARY
Literary Society

Ruth Fielding in Moving Pictures

Alice B. Emerson

© 1st World Library, 2007
PO Box 2211
Fairfield, IA 52556
www.1stworldlibrary.com
First Edition

LCCN: 2007935349

Softcover ISBN: 978-1-4218-9301-3
Hardcover ISBN: 978-1-4218-9401-0
eBook ISBN: 978-1-4218-9201-6

Purchase *"Ruth Fielding in Moving Pictures"*
as a traditional bound book at:
www.1stWorldLibrary.com/purchase.asp?ISBN=978-1-4218-9301-3

1st World Library is a literary, educational organization
dedicated to:

- Creating a free internet library of downloadable ebooks

- Hosting writing competitions and offering book publishing
scholarships.

Interested in more 1st World Library books? contact:
literacy@1stworldlibrary.com
Check us out at: www.1stworldlibrary.com

1ˢᵗ World Library Literary Society

Giving Back to the World

"If you want to work on the core problem, it's early school literacy."

- James Barksdale, former CEO of Netscape

"No skill is more crucial to the future of a child, or to a democratic and prosperous society, than literacy."

- Los Angeles Times

"Literacy... means far more than learning how to read and write... The aim is to transmit... knowledge and promote social participation."

- UNESCO

"Literacy is not a luxury, it is a right and a responsibility. If our world is to meet the challenges of the twenty-first century we must harness the energy and creativity of all our citizens."

- President Bill Clinton

"Parents should be encouraged to read to their children, and teachers should be equipped with all available techniques for teaching literacy, so the varying needs and capacities of individual kids can be taken into account."

- Hugh Mackay

CONTENTS

CHAPTER I

NOT IN THE SCENARIO

"What in the world are those people up to?"

Ruth Fielding's clear voice asked the question of her chum, Helen Cameron, and her chum's twin-brother, Tom. She turned from the barberry bush she had just cleared of fruit and, standing on the high bank by the roadside, gazed across the rolling fields to the Lumano River.

"What people?" asked Helen, turning deliberately in the automobile seat to look in the direction indicated by Ruth.

"Where? People?" joined in Tom, who was tinkering with the mechanism of the automobile and had a smudge of grease across his face.

"Right over the fields yonder," Ruth explained, carefully balancing the pail of berries. "Can't you see them, Helen?"

"No-o," confessed her chum, who was not looking at all where Ruth pointed.

"Where are your eyes?" Ruth cried sharply.

"Nell is too lazy to stand up and look," laughed Tom. "I see them. Why! there's quite a bunch—and they're running."

"Where? Where?" Helen now demanded, rising to look.

"Oh, goosy!" laughed Ruth, in some vexation. "Right ahead. Surely you can see them now?"

"Oh," drawled Tom, "sis wouldn't see a meteor if it fell into her lap."

"I guess that's right, Tommy," responded his twin, in some scorn. "Neither would you. Your knowledge of the heavenly bodies is very small indeed, I fear. What do they teach you at Seven Oaks?"

"Not much about anything celestial, I guarantee," said Ruth, slyly. "Oh! there those folks go again."

"Goodness me!" gasped Helen. "Where *are* these wonderful persons? Oh! I see them now."

"Whom do you suppose they are chasing?" demanded Tom Cameron. "Or, who is chasing *them*?"

"That's it, Tommy," scoffed his sister. "I understand you have taken up navigation with the other branches of higher mathematics at Seven Oaks; and now you want to trouble Ruth and me with conundrums.

"Are we soothsayers, that we should be able to explain, off-hand," pursued Helen, "the actions of such a crazy crowd of people as those—Do look there! that woman jumped right down that sandbank. Did you ever?"

"And there goes another!" Ruth exclaimed.

　　　　　Alice B. Emerson

"Likewise a third," came from Tom, who was quite as much puzzled as were the girls.

"One after the other—just like Brown's cows," giggled Helen. "Isn't that funny?"

"It's like one of those chases in the moving pictures," suggested Tom.

"Why, of course!" Ruth cried, relieved at once. "That's exactly what it is," and she scrambled down the bank with the pail of barberries.

"What is *what*?" asked her chum.

"Moving pictures," Ruth said confidently. "That is, it will be a film in time. They are making a picture over yonder. I can see the camera-man off at one side, turning the crank."

"Cracky!" exclaimed Tom, grinning, "I thought that was a fellow with a hand-organ, and I was looking for the monkey."

"Monkey, yourself," cried his sister, gaily.

"Didn't know but that he was playing for those 'crazy creeters'—as your Aunt Alvirah would call them, Ruthie—to dance by," went on Tom. "Come on! I've got this thing fixed up so it will hobble along a little farther. Let's take the lane there and go down by the river road, and see what it's all about."

"Good idea, Tommy-boy," agreed Ruth, as she got into the tonneau and sat down beside Helen.

"Fancy! taking moving pictures out in the open in mid-winter,"

Helen remarked. "Although this is a warm day."

"And no snow on the ground," chimed in Ruth. "Uncle Jabez was saying last evening that he doesn't remember another such open winter along the Lumano."

"Say, Ruthie, how does your Uncle Jabez treat you, now that you are a bloated capitalist?" asked Helen, pinching her chum's arm.

"Oh, Helen! don't," objected Ruth. "I don't feel puffed up at all—only vastly satisfied and content."

"Hear her! who wouldn't?" demanded Tom. "Five thousand dollars in bank—and all you did was to use your wits to get it. We had just as good a chance as you did to discover that necklace and cause the arrest of the old Gypsy," and the young fellow laughed, his black eyes twinkling.

"I never shall feel as though the reward should all have been mine," Ruth said, as Tom prepared to start the car.

"Pooh! I'd never worry over the possession of so much money," said Helen. "Not I! What does it matter how you got it? But you don't tell us what your Uncle Jabez thinks about it."

"I can't," responded Ruth, demurely.

"Why not?"

"Because Uncle Jabez has expressed no opinion—beyond his usual grunt. It doesn't really matter how the dear man feels," pursued Ruth Fielding, earnestly. "I know how *I* feel about it. I am no longer a 'charity child'—"

　　　　Alice B. Emerson

"Oh, Ruthie! you never were *that*," Helen hastened to say.

"Oh, yes I was. When I first came to the Red Mill you know Uncle Jabez only took me in because I was a relative and he felt that he *had* to."

"But you helped save him a lot of money," cried Helen. "And there was that Tintacker Mine business. If you hadn't chanced to find The Fox's brother out there in the wilds of Montana, and nursed him back to health, your uncle would never have made a penny in *that* investment."

Helen might have gone on with continued vehemence, had not Ruth stopped her by saying:

"That makes no difference in my feelings, my dear. Each quarter Uncle Jabez has had to pay out a lot of money to Mrs. Tellingham for my tuition. And he has clothed me, and let me spend money going about with you 'richer folks,'" and Ruth laughed rather ruefully. "I feel that I should not have allowed him to do it. I should have remained at the Red Mill and helped Aunt Alvirah—"

"Pooh! Nonsense!" ejaculated Tom, as the spark ignited and the engine began to rumble.

"You shouldn't be so popular, Ruth Fielding of the Red Mill," chanted Helen, leaning over to kiss her chum's flushed cheek.

"Look out for the barberries!" cried Ruth.

"I reckon you don't want to spill them, after working so hard to get them," Tom said, as the automobile lurched forward.

"I certainly do not," Ruth admitted. "I scratched my hands all up getting the bucket full. Just fancy finding barberries still clinging to the bushes in such quantities this time of the year."

"What good are they?" queried Helen, selecting one gingerly and putting it into her mouth.

"Oh! Aunt Alvirah makes the loveliest pies of them—with huckleberries, you know. Half and half."

"Where'll you find huckleberries this time of year?" scoffed Tom. "On the bushes too?"

"In glass jars down cellar, sir," replied Ruth, smartly. "I did help pick those and put them up last summer, in spite of all the running around we did."

"Beg pardon, Miss Fielding," said Tom. "Go on. Tell us some more recipes. Makes my mouth water."

"O-o-oh! so will these barberries!" exclaimed Helen, making a wry face. "Just taste one, Tommy."

"Many, many thanks! *Good*-night!" ejaculated her brother, "I know better. But those barberries properly prepared with sugar make a mighty nice drink in summer. Our Babette makes barberry syrup, you know."

"Ugh! It doesn't taste like these," complained his sister. "Oh, folks! there are those foolish actors again."

"*Now* what are they about?" demanded Ruth.

"Look out that you don't bring the car into the focus of the camera, Tom," his sister warned him. "It will make them awfully mad."

Alice B. Emerson

"Don't fret. I have no desire to appear in a movie," laughed Tom.

"But I think *I* would like to," said his sister. "Wouldn't you, Ruth?"

"I—I don't know. It must be awfully interesting—"

"Pooh!" scoffed Tom. "What will you girls get into your heads next? And they don't let girls like you play in movies, anyway."

"Oh, yes, they do!" cried his sister. "Some of the greatest stars in the film firmament are nothing more than school-girls. They have what they call 'film charm.'"

"Think you've got any of that commodity?" demanded Tom, with cheerful impudence.

"I don't know—Oh, Ruth, look at that girl! Now, Tommy, see there! That girl isn't a day older than we."

"Too far away to make sure," said Tom, slowly. Then, the next moment, he ejaculated: "What under the sun is she doing? Why! she'll fall off that tree-trunk, the silly thing!"

The slender girl who had attracted their attention had, at the command of the director of the picture, scrambled up a leaning sycamore tree which overhung the stream at a sharp angle. The girl swayed upon the bare trunk, balancing herself prettily, and glanced back over her shoulder.

Tom had brought the car to a stop. When the engine was shut off they could hear the director's commands:

"That's it, Hazel. Keep that pose. Got your focus, Carroll?"

he called to the camera man. "Now—ready! Register fear, Miss Hazel. Say! act as though you *meant* it! Register fear, I say—just as though you expected to fall into the water the next moment. Oh, piffle! Not at all like it! not at *all* like it!"

He was a dreadfully noisy, pugnacious man. Finally the girl said:

"If you think I am not scared, Mr. Grimes, you are very much mistaken. I *am*. I expect to slip off here any moment—Oh!"

The last was a shriek of alarm. What she was afraid would happen came to pass like a flash. Her foot slipped, she lost her balance, and the next instant was precipitated into the river!

Alice B. Emerson

CHAPTER II

THE FILM HEROINE

When the motion picture girl fell from the sycamore tree into the water, some of the members of the company, who sat or stood near by panting after their hard chase cross-lots, actually laughed at their unfortunate comrade's predicament.

But that was because they had no idea of the strength and treacherous nature of the Lumano. At this point the eddies and cross-currents made the stream more perilous than any similar stretch of water in the State.

"Oh, that silly girl!" shouted Mr. Grimes, the director. "There! she's spoiled the scene again. I don't know what Hammond was thinking of to send her up here to work with us.

"Hey, one of you fellows! go and fish her out. And that spoils our chance of getting the picture to-day. Miss Gray will have to be mollycoddled, and grandmothered, and what-not. Huh!"

While he scolded, the director scarcely gave a glance to the struggling girl. The latter had struck out pluckily for the shore when she came up from her involuntary plunge. After the cry she had uttered as she fell, she had not made a sound.

To swim with one's clothing all on is not an easy matter at the best of times. To do this in mid-winter, when the water is icy, is well nigh an impossibility.

Several of the men of the company, more humane than the director, had sprung to assist the unfortunate girl; but suddenly the current caught her and she was swerved from the bank. She was out of reach.

"And not a skiff in sight!" exclaimed Tom.

"Oh, dear! The poor thing!" cried his sister. "She's being carried right down the river. They'll never get her."

"Oh, Tom!" implored Ruth. "Hurry and start. *We must get that girl*!"

"Sure we will!" cried Tom Cameron.

He was already out of the car and madly turning the crank. In a moment the engine was throbbing. Tom leaped back behind the wheel and the automobile darted ahead.

The rough road led directly along the verge of the river bank. The picture-play actors scattered as he bore down upon them. It gave Tom, as well as the girls, considerable satisfaction to see the director, Grimes, jump out of the way of the rapidly moving car.

The friends in the car saw the actress, whom Grimes had called both "Hazel" and "Miss Gray," swirled far out from the shore; but they knew the current or an eddy would bring her back. She sank once; but she came up again and fought the current like the plucky girl she was.

"Oh, Helen! she's wonderful!" gasped Ruth, with clasped hands, as she watched this fight for life which was more thrilling than anything she had ever seen reproduced on the screen.

Helen was too frightened to reply; but Ruth Fielding often before had shown remarkable courage and self-possession in times of emergency. No more than the excited Tom did she lose her head on this occasion.

As has been previously told, Ruth had come to the banks of the Lumano River and to her Uncle Jabez Potter's Red Mill some years before, when she was a small girl. She was an orphan, and the crabbed and miserly miller was her single living relative.

The first volume of the series, entitled "Ruth Fielding of the Red Mill," tells of the incidents which follow Ruth's coming to reside with her uncle, and with Aunt Alvirah Boggs, who was "everybody's aunt" but nobody's relative.

The first and closest friends of her own age that Ruth made in her new home were Helen and Tom Cameron, twin children of a wealthy merchant whose all-year home was not far from the Red Mill. With Helen and Mercy Curtis, a lame girl, Ruth is sent to Briarwood Hall, a delightfully situated boarding school at some distance from the girls' homes, and there, in the second volume of the series, Ruth is introduced to new scenes, some new friends and a few enemies; but altogether has a delightful time.

Ensuing volumes tell of Ruth and her chums' adventures at Snow Camp; at Lighthouse Point; on Silver Ranch, in Montana; on Cliff Island, where occur a number of remarkable winter incidents; at Sunset Farm during the previous summer; and finally, in the eighth volume, the one immediately preceding this present story, Ruth achieves something that she has long, long desired.

This last volume, called "Ruth Fielding and the Gypsies; Or, The Missing Pearl Necklace," tells of an automobile trip which Ruth and her present companions, Helen and Tom Cameron, took through the hills some distance beyond the Red Mill and Cheslow, their home town.

They fall into the hands of Gypsies and the two girls are actually held captive by the old and vindictive Gypsy Queen. Through Ruth's bravery Helen escapes and takes the news of the capture back to Tom. Later the grandson of the old Gypsy Queen releases Ruth.

While at the camp Ruth sees a wonderful pearl necklace in the hands of the covetous old Queen Zelaya. Later, when the girls return to Briarwood, they learn that an aunt of one of their friends, Nettie Parsons, has been robbed of just such a necklace.

Ruth, through Mr. Cameron, puts the police on the trail of the Gypsies. The Gypsy boy, Roberto, is rescued and in time becomes a protege of Mr. Cameron, while the stolen necklace is recovered from the Gypsy Queen, who is deported by the Washington authorities.

In the end, the five thousand dollars reward offered by Nettie's aunt comes to Ruth. She is enriched beyond her wildest dreams, and above all, is made independent of the niggardly charity of her Uncle Jabez who seems to love his money more than he does his niece.

Unselfishness was Ruth's chief virtue, though she had many. She could never refuse a helping hand to the needy; nor did she fear to risk her own convenience, sometimes even her

　　　　　Alice B. Emerson

own safety, to relieve or rescue another.

In the present case, none knew better than Ruth the treacherous currents of the Lumano. It had not been so many months since she and her uncle, Jabez Potter, out upon the Lumano in a boat, had nearly lost their lives. This present accident, that to the young moving-picture actress, was at a point some distance above the Red Mill.

"If she is carried down two hundred yards farther, Tom, she will be swept out into mid-stream," declared Ruth, still master of herself, though her voice was shaking.

"And then—good-night!" answered Tom. "I know what you mean, Ruth."

"She will sink for the last time before the current sweeps her in near the shore again," Ruth added.

"Oh, don't!" groaned Helen. "The poor girl."

Tom had driven the automobile until it was ahead of the struggling Hazel Gray. An eddy clutched her and drew her swiftly in toward the bank. Immediately Tom shut off the power and he and Ruth both leaped out of the car.

A long branch from an adjacent tree had been torn off by the wind and lay beside the road. Tom seized this and ran with Ruth to the edge of the water; but he knew the branch was a poor substitute for a rope.

"If she can cling to this, I'll get something better in a moment, Ruth!" he exclaimed.

Swinging the small and bushy end of the branch outward, Tom dropped it into the water just ahead of the imperiled girl. Ruth seized the butt with her strong and capable hands.

"Cut off a length of that fence wire, Tommy," she ordered. "You have wire-cutters in your auto kit, haven't you?"

"Sure!" cried Tom. "Never travel without 'em since we were at Silver Ranch, you know. There! She's got it."

Hazel Gray had seized upon the branch. She was too exhausted to reach the bank of the river without help, and just here the eddy began to swing her around again, away from the shore.

The men of the company came running now, giving lusty shouts of encouragement, but—that was all! The director had allowed the girl to get into a perilous position on the leaning tree without having a boat and crew in readiness to pick her up if she fell into the river. It was an unpardonable piece of neglect, and there might still serious consequences arise from it.

For the girl in the water was so exhausted that she could not long cling to the limb. It was but a frail support between her and drowning.

When the men arrived Ruth feared to have them even touch the branch she held, and she motioned them back. She knew that the girl in the stream was almost exhausted and that a very little would cause her to lose her hold upon the branch altogether.

"Don't touch it! I beg of you, don't touch it!" cried Ruth, as one excited man undertook to take the butt of the branch.

"You can't hold it, Miss! you'll be pulled into the water."

Alice B. Emerson

"Never fear for me," the girl from the Red Mill returned. "I know what I am about—Oh, goody! here comes Tom!"

She depended on Tom—she knew that he would do something if anybody could. She gazed upon the wet, white face of the girl in the water and knew that whatever Tom did must be done at once. Hazel Gray was loosing her hold.

"Oh! oh! oh!" screamed Helen, standing in the automobile with clasped hands. "Don't let her drown, Tommy! Don't let her go down again— *don't*!"

Tom came, with grimly set lips, dragging about twenty feet of fence wire behind him. Luckily it was smooth wire—not barbed. He quickly made a loop in one end of it and wriggled the other end toward Ruth and the excited men.

"Catch hold here!" he ordered. "Make a loop as I have, and don't let it slip through your hands."

"Oh, Tom! you're never going into that cold water?" Ruth gasped, suddenly stricken with fear for her friend's safety.

But that was exactly what Tom intended to do. There was no other way. He had seen, too, the exhaustion of the girl in the water and knew that if her hands slipped from the tree branch, she could never get a grip on the wire.

Without removing an article of clothing the boy leaped into the stream. It was over his head right here below the bank, and the chill of the water was tremendous. As Tom said afterward, he felt it "clear to the marrow of his bones!"

But he came up and struck out strongly for the face of the girl, which was all that could be seen above the surface.

Hazel Gray's hold was slipping from the branch. She was blue about the lips and her eyes were almost closed. The current was tugging at her strongly; she was losing consciousness. If she was carried away by the suction of the stream, now dragging so strongly at her limbs, Tom Cameron would be obliged to loose his own hold upon the wire and swim after her. And the young fellow was not at all sure that he could save either her or himself if this occurred.

Yet, perilous as his own situation was, Tom thought only of that of the actress.

CHAPTER III

AT THE RED MILL

Helen, greatly excited, stood on the seat of the tonneau and cheered her brother on at the top of her voice. That, in her excitement, she thought she was "rooting" at a basket-ball game at Briarwood, was not to be wondered at. Ruth heard her chum screaming:

"S.B.—Ah-h-h!
S.B.—Ah-h-h
Sound our battle-cry
Near and far!
S.B.—All!
Briarwood Hall!
Sweetbriars, do or die—
This be our battle-cry—
Briarwood Hall!
That's All!"

At the very moment the excited Helen brought out the "snapper" of the rallying cry of their own particular Briarwood sorority, Ruth let the limb go, for Tom had seized the sinking actress by the shoulder.

"He's got her!" the men shouted in chorus.

"And that's all those fellows were," Ruth said afterwards, in some contempt. "Just a *chorus*! They were a lot of tabby-cats—afraid to wet their precious feet. If it hadn't been for Tom, Miss Gray would have been drowned before the eyes of that mean director and those other imitation men. Ugh! I de-*test* a coward!"

This was said later, however. Until they drew Tom and his fainting burden ashore, neither Ruth nor Helen had time for criticism. Then they bundled Hazel Gray in the automobile rugs, while Tom struggled into an overcoat and cranked up the machine. The director came to inquire:

"What are you going to do with that girl?"

"Take her to the Red Mill," snapped Ruth. "That's down the river, opposite the road to Cheslow. And don't try to see her before to-morrow. No thanks to *you* that she isn't drowned."

"You are a very impudent young lady," growled the director.

"I may be a plain spoken one," said Ruth, not at all alarmed by the man's manner. "I don't know how you would have felt had Miss Gray been drowned. I should think you would think of *that*!"

But the man seemed more disturbed about the delay to the picture that was being taken.

"I shall expect you to be ready bright and early in the morning, Miss Gray!" he shouted as the automobile moved off. The young actress, half fainting in the tonneau between the Briarwood Hall girls, did not hear him.

It was several miles to the Red Mill, and Ruth, worried, said: "I'm afraid Tom will catch cold, Helen."

Alice B. Emerson

"And—and this po—poor girl, too," stammered Tom's sister, as the car jounced over a particularly rough piece of road.

Hazel Gray opened her eyes languidly, murmuring: "I shall be all right, thank you! Just drive to the hotel—"

"What hotel?" asked Ruth, laughing.

"In Cheslow. I don't know the name of it," whispered Hazel Gray. "Is there more than one?"

"There is; but you'll not go all the way to Cheslow in your condition," declared Ruth. "We're taking you to the Red Mill. Now! no objections, please. Hurry up, Tommy."

"But I am all wet," protested the girl.

"I should say you were," gasped Helen.

"Nobody knows better than I," said Ruth, "that the water of the Lumano river is at least *damp*, at all seasons."

"I will make you a lot of trouble," objected Miss Gray.

"No, you won't," the girl of the Red Mill repeated. "Aunt Alvirah will snuggle you down between soft, fluffy blankets, and give you hot boneset tea, or 'composition,' and otherwise coddle you. To-morrow morning you will feel like a new girl."

"Oh, dear!" groaned Miss Gray. "I wish I *were* a new girl."

A very few minutes later they came in sight of the Red Mill, with the rambling, old, story-and-a-half dwelling beside it, in which Jabez Potter's grandfather had been born. Although the leaves had long since fallen from the trees, and the lawn was brown, the sloping front yard of the Potter house was very attractive. The walks were swept, the last dead leaf removed, and the big stones at the main gateway were dazzlingly white-washed.

The jar and rumble of the grist-mill, and the trickle of the water on the wheel, made a murmurous accompaniment to all the other sounds of life about the place. From the rear of the old house fowls cackled, a mule sent his clarion call across the fields, and hungry pigs squealed their prayer for supper. A cow lowed impatiently at the pasture bars in answer to the querulous blatting of her calf.

Tom was going on home to change his clothes; but when Ruth saw the fringe of icicles around the bottoms of his trouser legs, she would not hear to it.

"You come right in with us, Tom. Helen will drive the car home and get you a change of clothing. Meanwhile you can put on some of Uncle Jabez's old clothes. Hurry on, now, children!" and she laughingly drove Tom and Hazel Gray before her to the porch of the old house, where Aunt Alvirah, having heard the automobile, met them in amazement.

"What forever has happened, my pretty?" cried the little old lady, whose bent back and rheumatic limbs made her seem even smaller than she naturally was. "In the river? Do come in! Bring the young lady right into the best room, Ruthie. You strip off right before the kitchen fire, Master Tom. I'll bring you some things to put on. There's a huck towel on the nail yonder. Oh, my back! and oh, my bones!"

Thus talking, Aunt Alvirah hobbled ahead into the sitting room. The girl who had fallen into the river was now shivering. Ruth and the old lady undressed her as quickly as possible, and Aunt Alvirah made ready the bed with the

Alice B. Emerson

"fluffy" blankets in the chamber right off the sitting room.

"Do get one of your nighties for her, my pretty," directed Aunt Alvirah. "She wouldn't feel right sleepin' in one o' *my* old things, I know."

Ruth was excited. In the first place, as to most girls of her age, a "real live actress" was as much of a wonder as a Great Auk would have been; only, of course, Hazel Gray was much more charming than the garfowl!

Ruth Fielding was interested in moving pictures—and for a particular reason. Long before she had gained the reward for the return of the pearl necklace to Nettie Parsons' aunt, Ruth had thought of writing a scenario. This was not a very original thought, for many, many thousand other people have thought the same thing.

Occasionally, when she had been to a film show, Ruth had wondered why she could not write a playlet quite as good as many she saw, and get money for it. But it had been only a thought; she knew nothing about the technique of the scenario, or how to go about getting an opinion upon her work if she should write one.

Here chance had thrown her into the company of a girl who was working for the films, and evidently was of some importance in the moving picture companies, despite the treatment she had received from the unpleasant director, Mr. Grimes.

Ruth remembered now of having seen Hazel Gray upon the screen more than once within the year. She was regarded as a coming star, although she had not achieved the fame of many actresses for the silent drama who were no older.

So Ruth, feeling the importance of the occasion, selected from her store the very prettiest night gown that she owned —one she had never even worn herself—and brought it down stairs to the girl who had been in the river. A little later Hazel Gray was between Aunt Alvirah's blankets, and was sipping her hot tea.

"My dear! you are very, very good to me," she said, clinging to Ruth's hand. You and the dear little old lady. Are you as good to every stranger who comes your way?"

"Aunt Alvirah is, I'm sure," replied Ruth, laughing and blushing. Somehow, despite the fact that the young actress was only two or three years older than herself, the girl of the Red Mill felt much more immature than Miss Gray.

"You belittle your own kindness, I am sure," said Hazel. "And that *dear* boy who got me out of the river—Where is he?"

"Unseeable at present," laughed Ruth. "He is dressed in some of Uncle Jabez's clothing, a world too big for him. But Tom *is* one of the dearest fellows who ever lived."

"You think a great deal of him, I fancy?"

"Oh, yes, indeed!" cried Ruth, innocently. "His sister is my very dearest friend. We go to Briarwood Hall together."

"Briarwood Hall? I have heard of that. We go there soon, I understand. Mr. Hammond is to take some pictures in and around Lumberton."

"Oh!" exclaimed Ruth. 'That will be nice! I hope we shall see you up there, Miss Gray, for Helen and I go back to school in a week."

"Whether I see you there or not," said the young actress with a sigh, "I hope that I shall be able some time to repay you for what you do for me now. You are entirely too kind."

"Perhaps you can pay me more easily than you think," said Ruth, bashfully, but with dancing eyes.

"How? Tell me at once," said Miss Gray.

"I'm just *mad* to try writing a scenario for a moving picture," confessed Ruth. "But I don't know how to go about getting it read."

Miss Gray smiled, but made no comment upon Ruth's desire. She merely said, pleasantly:

"If you write your scenario, my dear, I will get our manager to read it."

"That awful Mr. Grimes?" cried Ruth. "Oh! I shouldn't want *him* to read it."

Hazel Gray laughed heartily at that. "Don't judge, the taste of a baked porcupine by his quills," she said. "Grimes is a very rough and unpleasant man; but he gets there. He is one of the most successful directors Mr. Hammond has working for him."

"You have mentioned Mr. Hammond before?" said Ruth, questioningly.

"He is the man I will show your scenario to." Then she added: "If I am still working for him. Mr. Hammond is a very nice man; but Grimes does not like me," and again the girl sighed, and a cloud came over her pretty face.

"I would not work under such a mean man as that Grimes!" declared Ruth. "You might have been drowned because of his carelessness."

"It is my misfortune—being an actress—often to work under unpleasant conditions. I want to get ahead, and I would like to please Grimes; he puts over his pictures, and he has made several film actresses quite famous. Of course, although my first consideration must necessarily be my bread and butter, I hope for a little fame on the side, too."

"Oh! you have achieved that, have you not?" said Ruth, timidly. "I thought you had already made a name for yourself."

"Not as great a name as I hope to gain some day," declared Hazel Gray. "But thank you for the compliment. I was carried on to the stage when I was a baby in arms by my dear mother, who was an actress of some ability. My father was an actor. He died of a fever in the South before I can remember, and when I was seven my mother died.

"Kind people trained me for the stage; they were kind enough to say I had talent. And now I have tried to do my best in the movies. Mr. Hammond thinks I am a good pantomimist; but Grimes declares I have no 'film charm,'" and Miss Gray sighed again. "He has another girl he wants to push forward, and is angry that Mr. Hammond did not send her to head this company."

"Then this Mr. Hammond is quite an important man?" asked Ruth.

"Head of the Alectrion Film Corporation. He is immensely wealthy and a really *good* man. Of course," went on Miss Gray, "he is in the business of making films for money; just the same, he makes a great many pictures purely for art's sake, or for educational reasons. You would like Mr. Hammond, I am sure," and the girl in bed sighed again.

Ruth saw that talking troubled Miss Gray and kept her mind upon her quarrel with the moving picture director; so it did not need Aunt Alvirah's warning to make the girl of the Red Mill steal away and leave the patient to such repose as she might get.

CHAPTER IV

A TIME OF CHANGE

Tom Cameron looked funny enough in some of the miller's garments; but he was none the worse for his bath in the river. He, too, had been dosed with hot tea by Aunt Alvirah, though he made a wry face over it.

"Never you mind, boy," Ruth told him, laughing. "It is better to have a bad taste in your mouth for a little while than a sore throat for a week."

"Hear! hear the philosopher!" cried Tom. "You'd think I was a tender little blossom."

"You know, you *might* have the croup," suggested Ruth, wickedly.

"Croup! What am I—a kid?" demanded Tom, half angry at this suggestion. He had begun to notice that his sister and Ruth were inclined to set him down as a "small boy" nowadays.

"How is it," Tom asked his father one day, "that Helen is all grown up of a sudden? *I'm* not! Everybody treats me just as they always have; but even Colonel Post takes off his hat to

Alice B. Emerson

our Helen on the street with overpowering politeness, and the other men speak to her as though she were as old as Mrs. Murchiston. It gets *me*!"

Mr. Cameron laughed; but he sighed thereafter, too. "Our little Helen *is* growing up, I expect. She's taken a long stride ahead of you, Tommy, while you've been asleep."

"Huh! I'm just as old as she is," growled Tom. "But *I* don't feel grown up."

And here was Ruth Fielding holding the same attitude toward him that his twin did! Tom did not like it a bit. He was a manly fellow and had always observed a protective air with Ruth and his sister. And, all of a sudden, they had become young ladies while he was still a boy.

"I wish Nell would come back with my duds," he grumbled. "I have a good mind to walk home in these things of the miller's."

"And be taken for an animated scarecrow on the way?" laughed Ruth. "Better 'bide a wee,' Tommy. Sister will get here with your rompers pretty soon. Have patience."

"Now you talk just like Bobbins' sister. Behave, will you?" complained Tom.

Ruth tripped out of the room to peep at the guest, and Aunt Alvirah hobbled in and, letting herself down into her low chair, with a groan of "Oh, my back! and oh, my bones!" smiled indulgently at Tom's gloomy face.

"What is the matter, Mister Tom?" she asked. "Truly, you look as colicky as Amos Dodge—an' they do say he lived on sour apples!"

Tom had to laugh at this; but it was rather a rueful laugh. "I don't know what is coming over these girls—Ruth and my sister," he said, "They're beginning to put on airs like grown ladies. Cracky! they used to be some fun."

"Growin' up, Mister Tom—growin' up. So's my pretty. I hate to see it, but ye can't fool Natur'—no, sir! Natur' says to these young things: 'Advance!' an' they've jest got to march, I reckon," and Aunt Alvirah sighed, too. Then her little, bird-like eyes twinkled suddenly and she chuckled. "Jest the same," she added, in a whisper, "Ruth got out all her doll-babies the other day and played with 'em jest like she was ten years old."

"Ho, ho!" cried Tom, his face clearing up. "I guess she's only making believe to be grown up, after all!"

Helen came finally and they left Tom alone in the kitchen to change his clothes. Then the Camerons hurried away, for it was close to supper time. Both Helen and Tom were greatly interested in the moving picture actress; but she had fallen into a doze and they could not bid her good-bye.

"But I'm going to run down in the morning to see how she is," Tom announced. "I'll see her before she goes away. She's a plucky one, all right!"

"Humph!" thought Ruth, when the automobile had gone, "Tom seems to have been wonderfully taken with that Miss Gray's appearance."

When Jabez Potter came in from the mill and found the strange girl in the best bed he was inclined to criticize. He was a tall, dusty, old man, for whom it seemed a hard task ever to speak pleasantly. Aunt Alvirah, when she was much put out with him, said he "croaked like a raven!"

Alice B. Emerson

"Gals, gals, gals!" he grumbled. "This house seems to be nigh full of 'em when you air to home, Niece Ruth."

"And empty enough of young life, for a fac', when my pretty is away," put in Aunt Alvirah.

Ruth, not minding her Uncle Jabez's strictures, went about setting the supper table with puckered lips, whistling softly. This last was an accomplishment she had picked up from Tom long ago.

"And whistling gals is the wust of all!" snarled Jabez Potter, from the sink, where he had just taken his face out of the soapsuds bath he always gave it before sitting down to table. "I reckon ye ain't forgot what I told ye:

'Whistlin' gals an' crowin' hens
Always come to some bad ends!'"

"Now, Jabez!" remonstrated Aunt Alvirah.

But Ruth only laughed. "You've got it wrong, Uncle Jabez," she declared. "There is another version of that old doggerel. It is:

"'Whistling girls and blatting sheep
Are the two best things a farmer can keep!'"

Then she went straight to him and, as his irritated face came out of the huck towel, she put both arms around his neck and kissed him on his grizzled cheek.

This sort of treatment always closed her Uncle Jabez's lips for a time. There seemed no answer to be made to such an argument—and Ruth *did* love the crusty old man and was grateful to him.

When the miller had retired to his own chamber to count and recount the profits of the day, as he always did every evening, Aunt Alvirah complained more than usual of the old man's niggardly ways.

"It's gittin' awful, Ruthie, when you ain't to home. He's ashamed to have me set so mean a table when you air here. For he *does* kinder care about what you think of him, my pretty, after all."

"Oh, Aunt Alvirah! I thought he was cured of *little* 'stingies.'"

"No, he ain't! no, he ain't!" cried the old lady, sitting down with a groan. "Oh, my back! and oh, my bones! I tell ye, my pretty, I have to steal out things a'tween meals to Ben sometimes, or that boy wouldn't have half enough to eat. Jabez has had a new padlock put on the meat-house door, and I can't git a slice of bacon without his knowin' on it."

"That is ridiculous!" exclaimed Ruth, who had less patience now than she once had for her great uncle's penuriousness. She was positive that it was not necessary.

"Ree-dic'lous or not; it's *so*," Aunt Alvirah asserted. "Sometimes I feel like I was a burden on him myself."

"*You* a burden, dear Aunt Alvirah!" cried Ruth, with tears in her eyes. "You would be a blessing, not a burden, in anybody's house. Uncle Jabez was very fortunate indeed to get you to come here to the Red Mill."

"I dunno—I dunno," groaned the old lady. "Oh, my back! and oh, my bones! I'm a poor, rheumaticky creeter—and nobody but Jabez would have taken me out o' the poorhouse an' done for me as he has."

"You mean, you have done for him!" cried Ruth, in some passion. "You have kept his house for him, and mended for him, and made a home for him, for years. And I doubt if he has ever thanked you—not *once*!"

"But I have thanked him, deary," said Aunt Alvirah, sweetly. "And I do thank him, same as I do our Father in Heaven, ev'ry day of my life, for takin' me away from that poorfarm an' makin' an independent woman of me a'gin. Oh, Jabez ain't all bad. Fur from it, my pretty—fur from it!

"Now that you ain't no more beholden to him for your eddication, an' all, he is more pennyurious than ever—yes he is! For Jabez's sake, I could almost wish you hadn't got all that money you did, for gittin' back the lady's necklace. Spendin' money breeds the itch for spendin' more. Since you wrote him that you was goin' to pay all your school bills, Jabez Potter is cured of the little itch of *that* kind he ever had."

"Oh, Aunt Alvirah! Think of me—I am glad to be independent, too."

"I know—I know," admitted Aunt Alvirah. "But it's hard on Jabez. He was givin' you the best eddication he could—"

"Grumblingly enough, I am sure!" interposed Ruth, with a pout. She could speak plainly to the little old woman, for Aunt Alvirah *knew*.

"Surely—surely," agreed the old lady. "But it did him good, jest the same. Even if he only spent money on ye for fear of what the neighbors would say. Opening his pocket for *your* needs, my pretty, was makin' a new man of Jabez."

"Dear me!" exclaimed Ruth, thinking it rather hard. "You

want me to be poor again, Aunt Alvirah."

"Only for your uncle's sake—only for his sake," she reiterated.

"But he can do more for Mercy Curtis," said Ruth. "He has helped her quite a little. He likes Mercy—better than he does me, I think."

"But he don't have to help Mercy no more," put in Aunt Alvirah, quickly. "Haven't you heard? Mercy's mother has got a legacy from some distant relative and now there ain't a soul on whom Jabez Potter thinks he's *got* to spend money. It's a terrible thing for Jabez—Meed an' it is, my pretty.

"Changes—changes, all the time! We were going on quite smooth and pleasant for a fac'. And *now*—Oh, my back! and oh, my bones!" and thus groaningly Aunt Alvirah finished her quite unusual complaint, for with all her aches and pains she was naturally a cheerful body.

CHAPTER V

"THAT'S A PROMISE"

The family at the Red Mill were early risers when the red, red sun threw his first rays across the frosty waters of the Lumano, Ruth Fielding's casement was wide open and she was busily tripping about the kitchen where her Uncle Jabez had built the fire in the range before going to the mill.

Ben, the hired man, was out doing the chores and soon brought two brimming pails of milk into the milk-room.

"Aunt Alviry will miss ye, Ruthie, when ye air gone back to school," Ben said bashfully, when Ruth, with capable air, began to strain the milk and pour it into the pans.

"Poor Aunt Alvirah!" sighed Ruth. "I hope you help her all you can when I'm not here, Ben?"

"I jest *do*!" said the big fellow, heartily. "T'tell the truth, Ruthie, sometimes I kin scarce a-bear Jabe Potter. I wouldn't work for him another month, I vow! if 'twasn't for the old woman—and—and *you*."

"Oh, thank you, Ben, for that compliment," cried Ruth, dimpling and running into the kitchen to set back the coffee-pot in which the coffee was threatening to boil over.

The breakfast dishes were not dried when the raucous "honk! honk! honk!" of an automobile horn sounded without. The machine stopped at the gate of the Potter house.

"My mercy! who kin that be?" demanded Aunt Alvirah, jerkily, and then settled back into her chair again by the window with a murmured, "Oh, my back! and oh, my bones!"

"It can't be Tom, can it?" gasped Ruth, running to the door. "So early—and to see Miss Gray?" for the thought that Tom Cameron was interested in the actress still stuck in Ruth's mind.

"It doesn't sound like Tom's horn," she added, as she struggled with the outer door. "Oh, dear! I *do* wish Uncle Jabez would fix this lock. There!"

The door flew open, and swung out, its weight carrying Ruth with it plump into the arms of a big man in a big fur coat which he had thrown open as he ascended the steps of the porch.

Ruth was almost smothered in the coat. And she would have slipped and fallen had not the stranger held her up, finally setting her squarely on her feet at arm's length, steadying her there and laughing the while.

"I declare, young lady," he said in a pleasant voice, "I did not expect to be met with such cordiality. Is this the way you always meet visitors at this beautiful, picturesque old place?"

"Oh, oh, oh! I—I—I—"

Alice B. Emerson

Ruth could only gasp at first, her cheeks ruddy with blushes, her eyes timid. Her tongue actually refused to speak two consecutive, sensible words.

"I must say, my dear," said the gentleman who, Ruth now saw, was a man as old as Mr. Cameron, "that you are as charming as the Red Mill itself. For, of course, this *is* the Red Mill? I was directed here from Cheslow."

"Oh, yes!" stammered Ruth. "This is the Red Mill. Did—did you wish to see Uncle Jabez?"

"Perhaps. But that was not my particular reason for coming here," said the stranger, laughing openly at her now. "I find his niece pleasanter to look at, I have no doubt; though Uncle Jabez may be a very estimable man."

Ruth was puzzled. She glanced past him to the big maroon automobile at the gate. Therein she saw the squat, pugnacious looking Mr. Grimes, and she jumped to a correct conclusion.

"Oh!" she cried faintly. "*you* are Mr. Hammond!"

"Perfectly correct, my dear. And who are you, may I ask?"

"Ruth Fielding. I live here, sir. We have Miss Gray with us."

"Quite so," said Mr. Hammond, nodding. "I have come to see Miss Gray—and to take her away if she is well enough to be moved."

"Oh, she is all right, Mr. Hammond. Only she is still lying in bed. Aunt Alvirah prevailed upon her to stay quiet for a while longer."

"And your Aunt Alvirah is probably right. But—may I come in? I'd like to ask you a few questions, even if Hazel is not to be seen as yet."

"Oh, certainly, sir!" cried Ruth, thus reminded of her negligence. "Do come in. Here, into the sitting room, please. It is warm in here, for Uncle Jabez kept a fire all night, and I just put in a good-sized chunk myself."

"Ah! an old-fashioned wood-heater, is it?" asked Mr. Hammond, following Ruth into the sitting room. "That looks like comfort. I remember stoking a stove like that when I was a boy."

Ruth liked this jolly, hearty, big man from the start. He was inclined to joke and tease, she thought; but with it all he had the kindliest manner and most humorous mouth in the world.

He turned to Ruth when the door was shut, and asked seriously: "My dear, is Miss Gray where she can hear us talk?"

"Why, no, sir," replied Ruth, surprised. "The door is shut— and it is a soundproof door, I am certain."

"Very well. I have heard Grimes' edition of the affair yesterday. Will you please give me *your* version of the accident? Of course, it *was* an accident?"

"Oh, yes, sir! Although that man ought not to have made her climb that tree—"

Mr. Hammond put up a warning hand, and smiled again. "I do not ask you for an opinion. Just for an account of what actually happened."

"But you intimated that perhaps Mr. Grimes was more at fault than he actually *was*," said Ruth, boldly. "Surely he did not push her off that tree!"

"No," said Mr. Hammond, drily. "Did she jump?"

"Jump! Goodness! do you think she is crazy?" demanded Ruth, so shocked that she quite forgot to be polite.

"Then she did not jump," the manager of the Alectrion Film Corporation said, quite placidly. "Very well. Tell me what you saw. For, I suppose, you were on the spot?"

"Yes, sir," said Ruth, not quite sure just then that the gentleman was altogether fair-minded. Later she understood that Mr. Hammond merely desired to get the stories of the accident from the observers with neither partiality nor prejudice.

Ruth repeated just what happened from the time she and her friends arrived in the Cameron car on the scene, till they reached the Red Mill and Miss Gray had been put to bed.

"Very clear and convincing. You are a good witness," declared Mr. Hammond, lightly; but she saw that the story had left an unpleasant impression on his mind. She did not see how he could blame the motion picture actress; but she feared that he did.

When Ruth tried to probe into that question, however, Mr. Hammond skilfully turned the subject to the picturesqueness of the Red Mill and its surroundings.

"This would make a splendid background for a film," he said, with enthusiasm. "We ought to have a story written around this beautiful old place, with all the romance and human interest that must be connected with the history of the house.

"Do you mind if we go out and look around a little? I would not disturb Miss Gray until she is perfectly rested and feels like rising."

"Surely I will show you around, sir!" cried Ruth. "Let me get my coat and hat."

She ran for her sweater and tam-o'-shanter, and joined Mr. Hammond on the porch. Mr. Hammond said nothing to Grimes, but allowed him to remain in the limousine.

Ruth took the moving picture magnate down to the shore of the river and showed him the wheel and the mill-side. The old stone bridge over the creek, too, was an object of interest. In fact, Ruth had thought so much about the situation of the Red Mill as a picture herself, that she knew just what would attract the gentleman's interest the most.

"I declare! I declare!" he murmured, over and over again. "It is better than I thought. A variety of scene, already for the action to be put into it! Splendid!"

"And I am sure," Ruth told him, "Uncle Jabez would not object to your filming the old place. I could fix it for you. He is not so difficult when once you know how to take him."

"I may ask your good offices in that matter," said Mr. Hammond. "But not now. Of course, Grimes could work up something in short order to fit these scenes here. He's excellent at that. But I think the subject is worthy of better treatment. I'd like a really big story, treated artistically, and one that would fit perfectly into the background of the Red Mill—nothing slapdash and carelessly written, or invented on the spur of the moment by a busy director—"

"Oh, Mr. Hammond!" cried Ruth, so excited now that she could no longer keep silent. "I'd dearly love to write a moving picture scenario about the old mill. And I've thought about it so much that I believe I could do it."

"Indeed?" said Mr. Hammond, with one of his queer smiles. "Did you ever write a scenario?"

"No, sir! but then, you know," said Ruth, naively, "one must always do a thing for the first time."

"Quite true—quite true. So Eve said when she bit into the apple," and Mr. Hammond chuckled.

"I would just *love* to try it," the girl continued, taking her courage in both hands. "I have a splendid plot—or, so I believe; and it is all about the Red Mill. The pictures would *have* to be taken here."

"Not in the winter, I fancy?" said Mr. Hammond.

"No, sir. When it is all green and leafy and beautiful," said Ruth, eagerly.

"Then," said Mr. Hammond, more seriously, "I'd try my 'prentice hand, if I were you, on something else. Don't write the Red Mill scenario now. Write some thrilling but simple story, and let me read it first—"

"Oh, Mr. Hammond!" gasped Ruth, with clasped hands. "Will you really *read* it?"

"Of course I will," laughed the gentleman. "No matter how bad it is. That's a promise. Here is my card with my private address upon it. You send it directly to me, and the first time I am at home I will get it and give it my best attention. That's a promise," he repeated.

"Oh, thank you, sir!" murmured Ruth delightedly, smiling and dimpling.

He pinched her cheek and his eyes grew serious for a moment. "I once knew a girl much like you, Miss Ruth," he said. "Just as full of life and enthusiasm. You are a tonic for old fogies like me."

"Old fogy!" repeated Ruth. "Why, I'm sure you are not old, Mr. Hammond."

"Never mind flattering me," he broke in, with assumed sternness. "Haven't I already promised to read your scenario?"

"Yes, sir," said Ruth, demurely. "But you haven't promised to produce it."

"Quite so," and he laughed. "But *that* only goes by worth. We will see what a schoolgirl like you can do in writing a scenario. It will give you practice so that you may be able to handle something really big about this beautiful old place. You know, now that the most popular writers of the day are turning their hands to movies, the amateur production has to be pretty good to 'get by,' as the saying is."

"Oh! now you are trying to discourage me."

"No. Only warning you," Mr. Hammond said, with another laugh. "I'll send you a little pamphlet on scenario preparation —it may help. And I hope to read your first attempt before long."

"Thank you, sir," Ruth responded. "And if ever I write my Red Mill scenario, I am going to write Miss Gray into it. She is just the one to play the lead."

"And she is a good little actress I believe," said Mr. Hammond. "I knew that Grimes had a girl that he wanted to push forward as the lead in this company he has up here. I never like to interfere with my directors if I can help it. But I will see that Miss Gray gets a square deal. She has had good training in the legitimate drama, she is pretty, and she has pluck and good breeding."

"That Mr. Grimes was horrid to her," repeated Ruth, casting a glance of dislike at the man in the limousine.

"Oh, well, my dear, we cannot make people over in this world. That is impossible. But I will take care that Hazel Gray gets a square deal. *That's* a promise, too, Ruth Fielding," and the gentleman laughed again.

CHAPTER VI

WHAT IS AHEAD?

While Ruth and Mr. Hammond had been walking about, the Camerons had come. Tom's automobile was parked just beyond the moving picture magnate's handsome limousine; and Tom had given more than one covetous glance at the big car before going into the house.

When Ruth returned and entered the big and friendly kitchen after ushering Mr. Hammond Into the sitting room again, she found the twins eagerly listening to and talking to Miss Hazel Gray, who was leisurely eating a late breakfast at the long table.

"Good morning, Ruth Fielding!" cried the guest, drawing her down to kiss her cheek. "You are a *dear*. I've been telling your friends so. I fancy one of them at least thoroughly agrees with me," and she cast a roguish glance at Tom.

Tom blushed and Helen giggled. Ruth turned kind eyes away from Tom Cameron and smiled upon Helen. "Yes," she said, demurely, "I am sure that Helen has been singing my praises. The girls are beginning to call her 'Mr. Boswell' at school. But I have heard complimentary words of you this morning, Miss Gray."

Alice B. Emerson

"Oh!" cried the young actress. "From Mr. Hammond?"

"Yes."

"He is a lovely man," declared Hazel Gray, enthusiastically. "I have always said so. If he would only make Grimes give me a square deal—"

"Those are the very words he used," interrupted Ruth, while Tom recovered from his confusion and Helen from her enjoyment of her twin's embarrassment. "He says you shall have a square deal."

While the young actress ate—and Aunt Alvirah heaped her plate, "killing me with kindness!" Hazel Gray declared—the young folk chattered. Ruth saw that Tom could scarcely keep his eyes off Miss Gray, and it puzzled the girl of the Red Mill.

Afterward, when Miss Gray had gone out with Mr. Hammond, and Tom was out of sight, Helen began to laugh. "Aren't boys funny?" she said to Ruth. "Tom is terribly smitten with that lovely Hazel Gray."

"Smitten?" murmured Ruth.

"Of course. Don't say you didn't notice it. He hasn't had a 'crush' on any girl before that I know of. But it's a sure-enough case of 'measles' *this* time. Busy Izzy tells me that most of the fellows in their class at Seven Oaks have a 'crush' on some moving picture girl; and now Tom, I suppose, will be cutting out of the papers every picture of Hazel Gray that he sees, and sticking them up about his room. And she has promised to send him a real cabinet photograph of herself in character in the bargain," and Helen laughed again.

But Ruth could not be amused about this. She was disturbed.

"I didn't think Tom would be so silly," she finally said.

"Pooh! it's nothing. Bobbins and Tom are getting old enough to cast sheep's eyes at the girls. Heretofore, Tommy has been crazy about the slapstick comedians of the movies; but I rather admire his taste if he likes this Hazel Gray. I really think she's lovely."

"So she is," Ruth said quite placidly. "But she is so much older than your brother—"

"Pooh! only two or three years. But, of course, Ruth, it's nothing serious," said the more worldly-wise Helen. "And boys usually are smitten with girls some years older than themselves—at first."

"Dear me!" gasped Ruth. "How much you seem to know about such things, Helen. *How did you find out?*"

At that Helen burst into laughter again. "You dear little innocent!" she exclaimed. "You're so blind—blind as a bat! You never see the boys at all. You look on Tom to-day just as though he were the same Tom that you helped find the time he fell off his bicycle and was hurt by the roadside. You remember? Ages and ages ago!"

But did Ruth look upon Tom Cameron in just that way? She said nothing in reply to Tom's sister.

They came out of the house together and joined Mr. Hammond and Miss Gray just as they were about to step into the limousine. Aunt Alvirah waved her hand from the window.

　　　　　Alice B. Emerson

"She's just lovely!" declared Miss Gray. "You should have met her, Mr. Hammond."

"That pleasure is in reserve," said the gentleman, smiling. "I hope to see the Red Mill again."

Tom came hurrying down to shake hands with Miss Gray. Ruth watched them with some puzzlement of mind. Tom was undoubtedly embarrassed; but the moving picture girl was too used to making an impression upon susceptible minds to be much disturbed by Tom Cameron's worship.

Mr. Hammond looked out of the door of the limousine before he closed it.

"Remember, Ruth Fielding, I shall be on the lookout for what you promised me."

"Oh, yes, sir!" Ruth cried, all in a flutter, for the moment having forgotten the scenario she proposed to write.

"That's a promise!" he said again gaily, and closed the door. The big car rolled away and left the three friends at the gateway.

"*What's* a promise, Ruth Fielding?" demanded her chum, with immense curiosity.

Ruth blushed and showed some confusion. "It's—it's a secret," she stammered.

"A secret from *me*?" cried Helen, in amazement.

"I—I couldn't tell even you, dearie, just now," Ruth said, with sudden seriousness. "But you shall know about it before anybody else."

"That Mr. Hammond is in it."

"Yes," admitted her chum. "That is just it. I don't feel that I can speak to anybody about it yet."

"Oh! then it's *his* secret?"

"Partly," Ruth said, her eyes dancing, for there and then, right at that very moment, she fell upon the subject for the first scenario she intended to submit to Mr. Hammond. It was "Curiosity"—a new version of Pandora's Box.

Helen was such a sweet-tempered girl that her chum's little mystery did not cause her more than momentary vexation.

Besides, their vacation time was now very short. Many things had to be discussed about the coming semester. At its end, in June, Ruth and Helen hoped to graduate from Briarwood Hall.

The thought of graduating from the school they loved so much was one of mingled pleasure and pain. Old Briarwood! where they had had so much fun—so many girlish sorrows—friends, enemies, struggles, triumphs, failures and successes! Neither chum could contemplate graduation lightly.

"If we go to college together, it will never seem like Briarwood Hall," Helen sighed. "College will be so *big*. We shall be lost among so many girls—some of them grown women!"

"Goodness!" laughed Ruth, suddenly, "we'll be almost 'grown women' ourselves before we get through college."

"Oh, don't!" exclaimed Helen. "I don't want to think of *that*."

What was ahead of the chums did trouble them. Their future school life was a mystery. There was no prophet to tell them of the exciting and really wonderful things that were to happen to them at Briarwood during the coming term.

CHAPTER VII

"SWEETBRIARS ALL"

"Oh, dear me!" complained Nettie Parsons, "I never can do it."

"'In the bright Lexicon of Youth, there is no such word as "fail,"'" quoted Mercy Curtis, grandiloquently.

"That must be a pretty poor reference book to have in one's library, then," said Helen, making fun of the old saying which the lame girl had repeated. "How do we know— perhaps there are other important words left out—*A bas le* Lexicon of Youth!"

"Perseverence is the winning game, Nettie," Ruth said to the Southern girl, cheerfully. "Stick to it."

"And if *then* you can't make the sum come right, come to Aunt Ruthie and *ask*. That's what *I* do," confessed Ann Hicks, the ranch girl.

"Perseverence wins," quoth Helen.

"Oh, it does, does it?" cried Jennie Stone, called by the girls "Heavy," in a smothered tone, for her mouth was full of

Alice B. Emerson

caramels. "Let me tell you that old 'saw' is a joke. My little kid cousin proved that the other day. She came to grandfather—who is just as full of maxims and bits of wisdom as Helen seems to be to-day, and the kid said:

"'Grandpa, that's a joke about "If at first you don't succeed," isn't it?'

"And her grandfather answered, 'Certainly not. "Try, try again." That's right.'"

"'Huh!' said the kid, who is one of these Cynthia-of-the-minute' youngsters, 'you're wrong, Grandpa. I've been working for an hour blowing soapbubbles and trying to pin them on a clothes line in the nursery to dry!' Perseverence didn't cut much of a figure in her case, did it?" finished Heavy, with a chuckle.

The crowd of girls was in the big "quartette" room in the West Dormitory of Briarwood Hall. The school had reopened only a week before, but all the friends were hard at work. All but Ann Hicks and Nettie Parsons hoped to graduate the coming June.

In the group, besides Ruth and Helen, were their room-mates, Mercy Curtis and Ann Hicks; Jennie Stone; Mary Cox, the red-haired girl usually called "The Fox;" and Nettie Parsons, "the sugar king's daughter," as she was known to the school. She was the one really rich girl at Briarwood—and one of the simplest in both manner and dress.

Nettie was backward in her studies, as was Ann Hicks. Nettie was a lovable, sweet-tempered girl, who had several reasons for being very fond of Ruth Fielding. Indeed, if the truth were told, not a girl in the quartette that afternoon but had some particular reason for loving Ruth.

Ruth's life at the school had been a very active one; yet she had never thrust herself forward. Although she had been the originator of the most popular—now the only sorority in the school, the Sweetbriars, she had refused to be its president for more than one term. All the older girls were "Sweetbriars" now.

Mercy Curtis, who had a sweet voice, now commenced to sing the marching song of the school, which had been adopted by the Sweetbriars and made over into a special sorority song. Sitting on her bed, with her arms clasped around her knees, the lame girl weaved back and forth as she sang:

> "'At Briarwood Hall we have many a lark—
> But one wide river to cross!
> The River of Knowledge—its current dark—
> Is the one wide river to cross!
> Sweetbriars all-l!
> One wide River of Knowledge!
> Sweetbriars all-l!
> One wide river to cross!
>
> "'Sweetbriars come here, one by one—
> But one wide river to cross!
> There's lots of work, but plenty of fun,
> With one wide river to cross!'"

"Altogether!" cried Heavy. "All join in!"

"The dear old chant!" said Helen, with a happy sigh.

Ruth had already taken up the chorus again, and her rich, full-throated tones filled the room:

> "'Sweetbriars all-l!

Alice B. Emerson

One wide River of Knowledge!
Sweetbriars all-l!
One wide river to cross!'"

"Once more!" exclaimed the girl from Montana, who could not herself sing a note in harmony, but liked to hear the others. The chant continued:

"'Sweetbriars joining, two by two—
There's one wide river to cross!
Some so scared they daren't say 'Booh!'
To the one wide river to cross!"

"That was *us*, Ruthie!" broke off Helen, laughing. "Remember how scared we were when we walked up the old Cedar Walk with The Fox, here, and didn't know whether we were going to be met with a brass band or a ticket to the guillotine?"

The Fox, otherwise Mary Cox, suddenly turned red. Ruth hastened to smooth over her chum's rather tactless speech, for Mary had been a different girl at that time from what she was now, and the memory of the hazing she had visited on Ruth and Helen annoyed her.

"And what did meet us?" cried Ruth, dramatically. "Why, a poor, emaciated creature standing at the steps of this old West Dormitory, complaining that she would starve before supper if the bell did not sound soon. You remember, Heavy?"

"And I feel that way now," said Jennie Stone in a hollow tone. "I don't know what makes me so, but I am continually hungry at least three times a day—and at regular intervals. I must see a physician about it."

"Aren't you afraid of the effect of eating so much, Jennie?" asked Helen, gently.

"What's that? Is there a new disease?" asked the fleshy girl, trying to express fear—which she never could do successfully in any such case. Jennie had probably never been ill in her life save as the immediate result of over-indulgence in eating.

"No, my dear," said Ruth Fielding's chum. "But they do tell me that eating *too* much may make one *fat*."

"Horrors!" ejaculated Jennie. "I can't believe you. Then that is what is the matter with me! I thought I looked funny in the mirror. I must be getting a wee bit plump."

"Plump!"

"Hear her!"

"She's the girl who went up in the balloon and came down 'plump!'"

The shouts that greeted Heavy's seriously put remark did not disturb the fleshy girl at all. "That is exactly the trouble," she went on, quite placidly. "And it cost me half a dollar yesterday."

"What's that?" asked somebody, curiously.

"Where?" asked another girl.

"In chapel. Didn't you see me trying to crawl through between the two rows of seats? And I got stuck!"

"Did you have to pay Foyle the fifty cents to pry you out,

Alice B. Emerson

Heavy?" demanded Ann Hicks.

"No. I dropped the half dollar and tried to find it. I looked for it; that's all I *could* do. I was too fat to find it."

"Did you look good, Jennie?" asked Ruth, sympathetically.

"Did I look good?" repeated the fleshy girl, with scorn. "I looked as good as a fat girl crawling around on all fours, ever *does* look. What do you think?"

The laugh at Jennie Stone's sally really cleared the room, for the warning bell for supper sounded almost immediately. Heavy and Nettie, and all who did not belong in the quartette room, departed. Then Mercy went tap, tap, tapping down the corridor with her canes—"just like a silly woodpecker!" as she often said herself; and Ann strode away, trying to hum the marching song, but ignominiously falling into the doleful strains of the "Cowboy's Lament" before she reached the head of the stairway.

"I really would like to know what that thing is you've been writing, Ruth," remarked Helen, when they were alone. "All those sheets of paper—Goodness! it's no composition. I believe you've been writing your valedictory this early."

"Don't be silly," laughed Ruth. "I shall never write the valedictory of this class. Mercy will do that."

"I don't care! Mrs. Tellingham considers you the captain of the graduating class. So now!" cried loyal Helen.

"That may be; but Mercy is our brilliant girl—you know that."

"Yes—the poor dear! but how could she ever stand up before

them all and give an oration?"

"She *shall*!" cried Ruth, with emphasis. "She shall *not* be cheated out of all the glory she wins—or of an atom of that glory. If she is our first scholar, she must, somehow, have all the honors that go with the position."

"Oh, Ruthie! how can you overcome her natural dislike of 'making an exhibition of herself,' as she calls it, and the fact that, really, a girl as lame as she is, poor creature, could never make a pleasant appearance upon the platform?"

"I do not know," Ruth said seriously. "Not now. But I shall think it out, if nobody else *can*. Mercy shall graduate with flying colors from Briarwood Hall, whether I do myself, or not!"

"Never mind," said Helen, laughing at her chum's emphasis. "At least the valedictorian will hail from this dear old quartette room."

"Yes," agreed Ruth, looking around the loved chamber with a tender smile. "What will we do when we see it no longer, Helen?"

"Oh, don't talk about it!" cried Helen, who had forgotten by this time what she had started to question Ruth about. "Come on! We'll be late for supper."

When her chum's back was turned, Ruth slipped out of her table drawer the very packet of papers Helen had spoken about. The sheets had been typewritten and were now sealed in a manila envelope, which was addressed and stamped.

Alice B. Emerson

She hesitated all day about dropping the packet in the mailbag; but now she took her courage in both hands and determined to send it to its destination.

CHAPTER VIII

A NEW STAR

Ruth had actually been trying her "prentice hand," as Mr. Hammond had called it, at the production of a moving picture scenario. It was the first literary work she had ever achieved, although her taste in that direction had been noted by Mrs. Tellingham and the under-instructors of the school.

Oh! she would not have had any of them know what she had done in secret since arriving at the Hall at the beginning of this term. She would not let even Helen know about it.

"If it is a success—if Mr. Hammond produces it—*then* I'll tell them," Ruth said to herself. "But if he tells me it is no good, then nobody shall ever know that I was so foolish as to attempt such a thing."

Even after she had it all ready she hesitated some hours as to whether or not she should send it to the address Mr. Hammond had given her. The pamphlet he had promised to send her had not arrived, and Ruth had little idea as to how a scenario should be prepared She had written much more explanatory matter than was necessary; but she had achieved one thing at least—she had been direct in the composition of her scenario and she had the faculty of saying just what she

Alice B. Emerson

meant, and that briefly. This concise style was of immense value to her, as Ruth was later to learn.

Ruth managed to slip the big envelope addressed to Mr. Hammond into the mailbag in the hall without spurring Helen's curiosity again. She had to chuckle to herself over it, for it really was a good joke on her chum.

Unconsciously, Helen had given her the idea for this little allegorical comedy which she had written. And how her friend would laugh if the picture of "Curiosity" should be produced and they should see it on the screen.

The girls crowded into the big dining room in an orderly manner, but with some suppressed whispering and laughter on the part of the more giggling kind. There were always some of the girls so full of spirits that they could not be entirely repressed.

The long tables quickly filled up. There were few beginners at this time of year, for most of the new scholars came to Briarwood Hall at the commencement of the autumn semester.

There was one new girl at the table where Ruth and her particular friends sat, over which Miss Picolet the little teacher of French, had nominal charge. Nowadays, Miss Picolet's life was an easy one. She had little trouble with even the more boisterous girls of the West Dormitory, thanks to the Sweetbriars.

The new pupil beside the French teacher was Amy Gregg. She was a colorless, flaxen-haired girl, with such light eyebrows and lashes that Helen said her face looked like a blank wall.

She was a nervous girl, too; she pouted a good deal and seemed dissatisfied. Of course, being a stranger, she was lonely as yet; but under the rules of the Sweetbriars she was not hazed. The S.B.'s word had become law in all such matters at Briarwood Hall.

After they were seated, Heavy Stone whispered to Ruth: "Isn't that Gregg girl the most discontented looking thing you ever saw? Her face would sour cream right now! I hope she doesn't overlook my supper and give me indigestion."

"Behave!" was Ruth's only comment.

There was supposed to be silence until all were served and the teachers began eating. The waitresses bustled about, light-footed and demure. Mrs. Tellingham, who was present on this evening, overlooked all from the small guest table, as it was called, placed at the head of the room on a slightly raised platform.

Mrs. Tellingham, Ruth thought, was the loveliest lady in the world. The girl of the Red Mill had never lost the first impression the preceptress had made upon her childish mind and heart when she had come to Briarwood Hall.

At last—just in time to save Heavy's life, it would seem—Miss Picolet lifted her fork and the girls began to eat. A pleasant interchange of conversation broke out:

"Did you hear what that funny little Pease girl said to Miss Brokaw in physiology class yesterday?" asked Lluella Fairfax, who was across the table from Ruth.

"No. What has the child said now? She's a queer little thing," Helen said, before her chum could answer.

"She's rather dense, don't you know," put in Lluella's chum, Belle Tingley.

"I'm not so sure of *that*," laughed Lluella. "Miss Brokaw became impatient with little Pease and said:

"'It seems you are never able to answer a question, Mary; why is it?'

"'If I knew all the things you ask me, Miss Brokaw,' said Pease, 'my mother wouldn't take the trouble to send me here.'"

"I'm sure *that* doesn't prove the poor little kiddie a dunce," laughed Ruth.

"Say! we have a dense one at this very table," hissed Heavy, a hand beside her mouth so that the sound of her whisper would not travel to the head of the table where Miss Picolet and the sullen looking new girl sat.

"What do you mean?" asked Belle, curiously.

"*Whom* do you mean?" added Helen.

"That infant yonder," hissed the fleshy girl.

"What about her?" Ruth asked. "I'm rather sorry for that little Gregg. She doesn't look happy."

"Say!" chuckled Heavy. "She tried for an hour yesterday to coax electricity into the bulb over her table, and then went to Miss Scrimp and asked for a candle. She got the candle, and burned it until one of the other girls looked in (you know she's not 'chummed' with anybody yet) and showed her where the push-button was in the wall. And at that," finished

Heavy, grinning broadly, "I'm not sure that she understood how the 'juice' was turned on. She must have come from the backwoods."

"Hush!" begged Ruth. "Don't let her think we're laughing at her."

"Miss Scrimp's very strict about candles and oil lamps," said Nettie. "We use them a lot in the South."

"That old house of yours in 'So'th Ca'lina' must be a funny old place, Nettie," said Heavy.

"It isn't ours," Nettie said. "The cotton plantation belongs to Aunt Rachel. She was born on it—the Merredith Place. We usually go there for the early summer, and then either come No'th, or into the mountains of Virginia until cool weather. My own dear old Louisiana home isn't considered healthy for us during the extreme hot weather. It is too damp and marshy."

"'Way down Souf in de land ob cotton—
Cinnamon seed an' sandy bottom!'"

hummed Heavy. "Oh! I wish I was in Dixie—right now."

"Wait till my Aunt Rachel comes up here," Nettie promised. "I'm going to beg an invitation for you girls to visit Merredith."

"But it will be hot weather, then," said Heavy; "and I don't want to miss Light-house Point."

"And I'm just about crazy to get back to Silver Ranch," said Ann Hicks.

Alice B. Emerson

"Me for Cliff Island," cried Belle Tingley. "No land of cotton for mine, this summer."

"When is your aunt coming, Nettie?" asked Ruth.

"To see you graduate, my dear," replied the Southern girl, smiling. "And wait till she meets you, Ruthie Fielding! She'll near about love you to death!"

"Oh, everybody loves Ruth. Why shouldn't they?" cried Belle.

"But everybody doesn't give her a fortune, as Nettie's Aunt Rachel did," laughed Heavy.

Ruth wished they would not talk so much about that money; but, of course, she could not stop them. She made no rejoinder, but looked across the room and out at the upper pane of one of the long windows. It was deep dusk now without. The evening was clear, with a rising wind moaning through the trees on the campus.

Tony Foyle, the old gardener and general handy man, was only now lighting the lamps along the walks.

"There's a funny red star," Ruth said to Helen. "It can't be that Mars is rising *there*."

"Where?" queried her chum, lazily, scarcely raising her eyes to look. Helen was not interested in astronomy.

Nobody else was attracted by the red spark Ruth saw. Against the dusky sky it grew swiftly A new star—

"It is fire!" gasped Ruth, softly, rising on trembling limbs. "*And it is in the West Dormitory*!"

CHAPTER IX

THE DEVOURING ELEMENT

Not even Helen heard Ruth's whispered words. She went on calmly with her supper when her chum arose from her seat.

Ruth quickly controlled herself. The word "fire" would start a panic on the instant, although both dormitories were across the campus from the main hall.

The girl of the Red Mill erased from her countenance all expression of the fear which gripped her; but about her heart she felt a pressure like that of a tight band. Her knees actually knocked together; she was thankful they were invisible just then.

When she started up the room toward Mrs. Tellingham's table Ruth walked steadily enough. Some of the girls looked after her in surprise; but it was not an uncommon thing for a girl to leave her seat and approach the preceptress.

Mrs. Tellingham looked up with a smile when she saw Ruth coming. She always had a smile for the girl of the Red Mill.

The preceptress, however, was a sharp reader of faces. Her own expression of countenance did not change, for other

Alice B. Emerson

girls were looking; but she saw that something serious had occurred.

"What is it, Ruth?" she asked, the instant her low whisper could reach Ruth's ear.

The girl, looking straight at her, made the letters "F-I-R-E" with her lips. But she uttered no sound. Mrs. Tellingham understood, however, and demanded:

"Where?"

"West Dormitory, Mrs. Tellingham," said Ruth, coming closer.

"Are you positive?"

"I can see it from my seat. On the second floor. In one of the duo rooms at this side."

Ruth spoke these sentences in staccato; but her voice was low and she preserved an air of calmness.

"Good girl!" murmured Mrs. Tellingham. "Go out quietly and then run and tell Tony. Do you know where he is?"

"Lighting the lamps," whispered Ruth.

"Good. Tell him to go right up there and see what can be done. Warn Miss Scrimp. I will telephone to town, and Miss Brokaw will take charge and march the pupils to the big hall to call the roll. I hope nobody is in the dormitories."

Mrs. Tellingham had pushed back her chair and dropped her napkin; but her movements, though swift, were not alarming. She passed out by a rear door which led to the kitchens, while Ruth walked composedly down the room to the main exit.

"Hey! what's the matter, Ruthie?" called Heavy, in a low tone. "Whose old cat's in the well?"

Ruth appeared not to hear her. Miss Brokaw, a very capable woman, came into the dining hall as Ruth passed out. Miss Brokaw stepped to the monitor's desk at one side and tapped on the bell.

"Oh, mercy!" gasped Heavy, the incorrigible. "She's shut us off again. And I haven't had half enough to eat."

"Rise!" said Miss Brokaw, after a moment of waiting. "Immediately, girls. Miss Stone, you will come, too."

A murmur of laughter rose at Jennie Stone's evident intention to linger; but Heavy always took admonition in good part, and she arose smiling.

"Monitors to their places," commanded Miss Brokaw. "You will march to the big hall. It is Mrs. Tellingham's request. She will have something of importance to say to you."

The big hall was on the other side of the building, and from its windows nothing could be seen of either dormitory.

Meanwhile, Ruth, once alone in the hall, had bounded to the chief entrance of the building and opened one leaf of the heavy door. It was a crisp night and the frost bit keenly. The wind fluttered her skirt about her legs.

She stopped for no outer apparel, however, but dashed out upon the stone portico, drawing the door shut behind her. That act alone saved the school from panic; for it she had left the door ajar, when the girls filed out into the entrance hall from the dining room some of them would have been sure to see the growing red glow on the second floor of the West Dormitory.

To Ruth the fire seemed to be filling the room in which it had apparently started. There was no smoke as yet; but the flames leaped higher and higher, while the illumination grew frightfully.

A spark of light coming into being at the far end of the campus near the East Dormitory, showed Ruth where Tony Foyle then was. He was not likely to see the fire as yet, for in lighting the campus lamps he followed a route that kept his back to the West Dormitory until he turned to come back.

Like an arrow from the bow the young girl ran toward the distant gardener. She took the steps of the little Italian garden in the center of the campus in two flying leaps, passed the marble maiden at the fountain, and bounded up to the level of the campus path again without stopping.

"Tony! Oh, Tony!" she called breathlessly.

"Shure now, phat's the matter widyer?" returned the old Irishman, querulously. "Phy! 'tis Miss Ruth, so ut is. Phativer do be the trouble, me darlin'?"

He was very fond of Ruth and would have done anything in his power for her. So at once Tony was exercised by her appearance.

"Phativer is the matter?" he repeated.

"Fire!" blurted out Ruth, able at last to speak. The keen night air had seemed for the moment fairly to congest her lungs and render her speechless and breathless.

"That's *that*?" cried Tony. "'Fire,' says you? An' where is there fire save in the furnaces and the big range in the kitchen—"

He had turned, and the red glare from the room on the second floor of the West Dormitory came into his view.

"There it is!" gasped Ruth, and just then the tinkle of breaking glass betrayed the fact that the heat of the flames was bursting the panes of the window.

"Fur the love of—Begorra! I'll git the hose-cart, an' rouse herself an' the gals in the kitchen—"

Poor Tony, so wildly excited that he dropped the little "dhudeen" he was smoking and did not notice that he stepped on it, galloped away on rheumatic legs. At this hour there was no man on the premises but the little old Irishman, who cared for the furnaces until the fireman and engineer came on duty at seven in the morning.

Ruth was quite sure that neither Tony nor "herself" (by this name he meant Mrs. Foyle, the cook) or any of the kitchen girls, could do a thing towards extinguishing the fire. But she remembered that Miss Scrimp, the matron, must be in the threatened building, and the girl dashed across the intervening space and in at the door.

There was not a sound from upstairs—no crackling of flames. Ruth would never have believed the dormitory was afire had she not seen the fire outside.

The girl ran down the corridor to Miss Scrimp's room, and burst in the door like a young hurricane. The matron was at

Alice B. Emerson

tea, and she leaped up in utter amazement when she saw Ruth.

"For the good land's sake, Ruthie Fielding!" she ejaculated. "Whatever is the matter with you?"

"Fire!" cried Ruth. "One of the rooms on the next floor—front—is all afire! I saw it from the dining hall! Mrs. Tellingham has telephoned for the department at Lumberton—"

With a shriek of alarm, Miss Scrimp picked up the little old "brown Betty" teapot off the hearth of her small stove, and started out of the room with it—whether with the expectation of putting out the fire with the contents of the pot, or not, Ruth never learned.

But when the lady was half way up the first flight of stairs the flames suddenly burst through the doorframe, and Miss Scrimp stopped.

"That candle!" she shrieked. "I knew I had no business to give that girl that candle."

"Who?" asked Ruth.

"That infant—Amy Gregg her name is. I'll tell Mrs. Tellingham—"

"But please don't tell anybody else, Miss Scrimp," begged Ruth. "It will be awful for Amy if it becomes generally known that she is at fault."

"Well, now," said the matron more calmly, coming down the stairs again. "You are right, Ruthie—you thoughtful child. We can't do a thing up there," she added, as she reached the lower floor again. "All we can do is to take such things out as we can off this floor," and she promptly marched out with the little tea-pot and deposited it carefully on the grassplot right where somebody would be sure to step on it when the firemen arrived.

Miss Scrimp prided herself upon having great presence of mind in an emergency like this. A little later Ruth saw the good woman open her window and toss out her best mirror upon the cement walk.

Miss Picolet came flying toward the burning building, chattering about her treasures she had brought from France. "Le Bon Dieu will not let to burn up my mothair's picture—my harp—my confirmation veil—all, all I have of my youth left!" chattered the excited little Frenchwoman, and because of her distress and her weakness, Ruth helped remove the harp and likewise the featherbed on which the French teacher always slept and which had come with her from France years before.

By the time these treasures were out of the house a crowd came running from the main building—Mrs. Foyle, some of the kitchen girls and waitresses, Tony dragging the hose cart, and last of all Dr. Tellingham himself.

The good old doctor was the most absent minded man in the world, and the least useful in a practical way in any emergency. He never had anything of importance to do with the government of the school; but he sometimes gave the girls wonderfully interesting lectures on historical subjects. He wrote histories that were seldom printed save in private editions; but most of the girls thought the odd old gentleman a really wonderful scholar.

He was in dishabille just now. He had run out in his

Alice B. Emerson

dressing-gown and carpet slippers, and without his wig. That wig was always awry when he was at work, and it was a different color from his little remaining hair, anyway. But without the toupe at all he certainly looked naked.

"Go back, that's a dear man!" gasped Mrs. Foyle, turning the doctor about and heading him in the right direction. "Shure, ye air not dacently dressed. Go back, Oi say. Phat will the young ladies be thinkin' of yez? Ye kin do no good here, dear Dochter."

This was quite true. He could do no good. And, as it turned out later, the unfortunate, forgetful, short-sighted old gentleman had already done a great deal of harm.

CHAPTER X

GAUNT RUINS

Ruth Fielding felt a strong desire to return to the threatened building, and to make her way upstairs to that old quartette room she and her chums had occupied for so long. There were so many things she desired to save.

Not alone were there treasures of her own, but Ruth knew of articles belonging to her chums that they prized highly. It seemed actually wicked to stand idle while the hot flames spread, creating a havoc that nobody could stay.

Why! if the firemen did not soon appear, the whole West Dormitory would be destroyed.

The burst of smoke and flame into the corridor at the top of the front flight of stairs shut off any attempt to reach the upper stories from this direction. And although the back door of the building was locked, Ruth knew she could run down the hall, past Miss Scrimp's already gutted room, and up the rear stairway.

But when she started into the building again, Miss Scrimp screamed to her:

Alice B. Emerson

"Come out of that, you reckless girl! Don't dare go back for anything more of mine or Miss Picolet's. If we lose them, we lose them; that's all."

"But I might get some things of my own—and some belonging to the other girls."

"Don't *dare* go into the building again," commanded Miss Scrimp. "If you do, Ruthie Fielding, I'll report you to Mrs. Tellingham."

"Shure, she won't go in and risk her swate life," said Mrs. Foyle. "Come back, now, darlin'. 'Tis a happy chance that none o' the young leddies bes up there in thim burnin' rooms, so ut is."

"Oh, dear me! oh, dear me!" gasped Miss Picolet. "I presume it is *posi-tive* that there is nobody up there? Were all the mesdemoiselles at supper this evening?"

"Yes, yes," said Mrs. Tellingham's own voice. "Miss Brokaw has called the roll and there is none missing but our Ruthie. And now *you* would better run back, my dear," she added to Ruth. "You have no wrap or hat. I fear you will take cold."

"I never noticed it," confessed Ruth. "I guess the excitement kept me warm. But oh! how awful It is to see the old dormitory burn—and all our things in it."

"We cannot help it," sighed the principal. "Go up to the hall with the other girls, my dear. Here come the firemen. You may be hurt here."

The galloping of horses, blowing of horns, and shouting of excited men, now became audible. The glare of the fire could probably be seen by this time clear to Lumberton, and half the population of the suburbs on this side of the town would soon be on the scene.

Not until the firemen actually arrived did the girls in the big hall know what had happened. There had been singing and music and a funny recitation by one girl, to while away the time until Mrs. Tellingham appeared. Just as Ruth came in, her chum had her violin under her chin and was drawing sweet sounds from the strings, holding the other girls breathless.

But the violin music broke off suddenly and several girls uttered startled cries as the first of the fire trucks thundered past the windows.

"Oh!" shrieked somebody, "there is a fire!"

"Quite true, young ladies!" exclaimed Miss Brokaw, tartly. "And it is not the first fire since the world began. Ruth has just come from it. She will tell you what it is all about."

"Oh, Ruth!" cried Helen. "Is it the dormitory?"

"Give her time to speak," commanded the teacher.

"Which dormitory?" cried Heavy Stone.

"Now, be quiet—do," begged Ruth, stepping upon the platform, and controlling herself admirably. "Don't scream. None of us can do a thing. The firemen will do all that can be done"

"They'll about save the cellar. They always do," groaned the irrepressible Heavy.

"It is our own old West Dormitory," said Ruth, her voice

shaking. "Nothing can be taken from the rooms upstairs. Only some of Miss Scrimp's and Miss Picolet's things were saved."

"Oh, dear me!" cried Helen. "We're orphans then. I'm glad I had my violin over here!"

"Is everything going to be really burned up?" demanded Heavy. "You don't mean *that*, Ruth Fielding?"

"I hope not. But the fire has made great head-way."

"Oh! oh! oh!" were the murmured exclamations.

"Won't our dormitory burn, too?" demanded one of the East Dormitory girls.

But there was no danger of that. The wisdom of erecting the two dormitories so far apart, and so far separated from the other buildings, was now apparent. Despite the high wind that prevailed upon this evening, there was no danger of any other building around the campus being ignited.

Miss Brokaw had some difficulty in restoring order. Several of the girls were in tears; their most valued possessions were even then, as Heavy said, "going up in smoke."

Very soon practical arrangements for the night were under way. Unable to do anything to help save the burning structure, Mrs. Tellingham had returned to the main building, and the maids from the kitchen were soon bringing in cots and spare mattresses and arranging them about the big hall for the use of the girls.

The East Dormitory girls were asked to sit forward. ("The goats were divided from the sheep," Helen said.) Then the houseless girls were allowed to "pitch camp," as it were.

"It *is* just like camping out," cried Belle Tingley.

"Only there's no scratchy and smelly balsam for beds, and our clothes won't get all stuck up with chewing gum," said Lluella Fairfax.

"Chewing gum! Hear the girl," scoffed Ann Hicks. "You mean spruce gum."

"Isn't that about the same?" demanded Lluella, with some spirit. "You chew it, don't you?"

"I don't know. I wouldn't chew spruce gum unless it was first properly prepared. I tried it once," replied Ann, "and got my jaws so gummed up that I might as well have had the lockjaw."

"It is according to what season you get the gum," explained Helen. "Now, see here, girls: We ought to have a name for this camp."

"Oh, oh!"

"Quite so!"

"'Why not?" were some of the responses to this suggestion.

"Let's call it 'Sweet Dreams,'" said one girl. "That's an awfully pretty name for a camp, I think. We called ours that, last summer on the banks of the Vingie River."

"Ya-as," drawled Heavy. "Over across from the soap factory. I know the place. 'Sweet Dreams,' indeed! Ought to have called it 'Sweet Smells,'"

"I think 'Camp Loquacity' will fit *this* camp better," Ruth said bluntly. "We all talk at once. Goodness! how does *one* person ever get a sheet smooth on a bed?"

Helen came to help her, and just then Mrs. Tellingham herself appeared in the hall.

"I am glad to announce, girls," she said, with some cheerfulness, "that the fire is under control."

"Oh, goody!" cried Heavy. "Can we go over there to sleep to-night?"

"No. Nor for many other nights, if at all," the preceptress said firmly. "The West Dormitory is badly damaged. Of course, no girl need expect to find much that belongs to her intact. I am sorry. What I can replace, I will. We must be cheerful and thankful that no life was lost."

"What did I tell you?" muttered the fleshy girl. "Those firemen from Lumberton always save the cellar."

"Now," said Mrs. Tellingham, "the girls belonging in the East Dormitory will form and march to their rooms. It is late enough. We must all get quiet for the night. The ruins will wait until morning to be looked at, so I must request you to go directly to bed."

Somebody started singing—and of course it was their favorite, "One Wide River," that they sang, beginning with the very first verse. The words of the last stanza floated back to the West Dormitory girls as the others marched across the campus:

"'Sweetbriars enter, ten by ten—
That River of Knowledge to cross!

They never know what happens then,
With one wide river to cross!
One wide river!
One wide River of Knowledge!
One wide river!
One wide river to cross.'"

"But just the same it's no singing matter for us," grumbled Belle. "Turned out of our beds to sleep this way! And all we've lost!" She began to weep. It was difficult for even Heavy to coax up a smile or to bring forth a new joke.

Ruth and her chums secured a corner of the great room, and they insisted that Mercy Curtis have the single cot that had been secured.

"I don't mind it much," Ann Hicks declared. "I've camped out so many times on the plains without half the comforts of this camp. Oh! I could tell you a lot about camping out that you Easterners have no idea of."

"Postpone it till to-morrow, please, Miss Hicks," said Miss Brokaw, dryly. "It is time for you all to undress."

After they were between the sheets Helen crept over to Ruth and hid her face upon her chum's shoulder, where she cried a few tears.

"All my pretty frocks that Mrs. Murchiston allowed me to pick out! And my books! And—and—"

The tragic voice of Jennie Stone reached their ears: "Oh, girls! I've lost in the dreadful fire the only belt I could wear. It's a forty-two."

There was little laughter in the morning, however, when the

Alice B. Emerson

girls went out-of-doors and saw the gaunt ruins of the dear old West Dormitory.

The roof had fallen in. Almost every pane of glass was broken. The walls had crumbled in places, and over all was a sheet of ice where the cascades from the firemen's hose had blanketed the ruins.

It needed only a glance to show that to repair the building was out of the question. The West Dormitory must be constructed as an entirely new edifice.

CHAPTER XI

ONE THING THE OLD DOCTOR DID

Every girl in Briarwood Hall was much troubled by the result of the fire. The old rivalry between the East and the West Dormitories, that had been quite fierce at times and in years before, had died out under Ruth Fielding's influence.

Indeed, since the inception of the Sweetbriars a better spirit had come over the entire school. Mrs. Tellingham in secret spoke of this as the direct result of Ruth's character and influence; for although Ruth Fielding was not namby-pamby, she was opposed to every form of rude behavior, or to the breaking of rules which everyone knew to be important.

The old forms of hazing—even the "Masque of the Marble Harp," as it was called—were now no longer honored, save in the breach. The initiations of the Sweetbriars were novel inventions—usually of Ruth's active brain; but they never put the candidate to unpleasant or risky tasks.

There certainly were rivalries and individual quarrels and sometimes clique was arrayed against clique in the school. This was a school of upwards of two hundred girls—not angels.

Alice B. Emerson

Nevertheless, Mrs. Tellingham and the instructors noted with satisfaction how few disturbances they had to settle and quarrels to take under advisement. This class of girls whom they hoped to graduate in June were the most helpful girls that had ever attended Briarwood Hall.

"The influence of Ruth and some of her friends has extended to our next class as well," Mrs. Tellingham had said. "Nettie Parsons and Ann Hicks will be of assistance, too, for another year. I wish, however, that Ruth Fielding's example and influence might continue through *my* time—I certainly do."

The girls of the East Dormitory held a meeting before breakfast and passed resolutions requesting Mrs. Tellingham to rearrange their duo and quartette rooms so that as many as possible of the West Dormitory girls could be housed with them.

"We're all willing to double up," said Sarah Fish, who had become leader of the East Dormitory. "I'm perfectly willing to divide my bureau drawers, book-shelves, table and bed with any of you orphans. Poor things! It must be awful to be burned out."

"Some of us haven't much to put in bureau drawers or on bookshelves," said Helen, inclined to be lugubrious. "I—I haven't a decent thing to wear but what I have on right now. I unpacked my trunk clear to the very bottom layer."

However, as a rule, selfish considerations did not enter into the girls' discussion of the fire. When they looked at the ruined building, they saw mainly the loss to the school. A loyalty is bred in the pupils of such an institution as Briarwood Hall, which is only less strong than love of home and country.

A new structure to house a hundred girls would cost a deal of money.

There was no studying done before breakfast the morning after the fire; and at the tables the girls' tongues ran until Miss Brokaw declared the room sounded like a great rookery she had once disturbed near an old English rectory.

"I positively cannot stand it, young ladies," declared the nervous teacher, who had been up most of the night. "Such continuous chatter is enough to crack one's eardrums."

The girls really were too excited to be very considerate, although they did not mean to offend Miss Brokaw. If the window or an outer door was opened, the very tang of sour smoke on the air set their tongues off again about the fire.

Once in chapel, however, a rather solemn feeling fell upon them. The teacher whose turn it was to read, selected a psalm of gratitude that seemed to breathe just what was in all their hearts. It gave thanks for deliverance from the terrors of the night and those of the noonday, for the Power that encircles poor humanity and shelters it from harm.

"We, too, have been sheltered," thought Ruth and her friends. "We have been guarded from the evil that flyeth by night and from the terror that stalketh at noonday. Surely God is our Keeper and Strength. We will not be afraid."

When Helen played one of the old, old hymns of the Church she brought such sweet tones from the strings of the violin that Miss Picolet hushed her accompaniment, surprised and delighted. And when they sang, Ruth Fielding's rich and mellow voice carried the air in perfect harmony.

When the hymn was finished the girls turned glowing faces

upon Mrs. Tellingham who, despite a sleepless night, looked fresh and sweet.

"For the first time in the history of Briarwood Hall as a school," she said, speaking so that all could hear her, "a really serious calamity has fallen."

"We are all determined upon one thing, I am sure," pursued Mrs. Tellingham. "We will not worry about what is already done. Water that has run by the mill will never drive the wheel, you know. We will look forward to the rebuilding of the West Dormitory, and that as soon as it can possibly be done."

"Hoo-ray!" cried Jennie Stone, leading a hearty cheer.

"We will have the ruin of the old structure torn away at once."

The murmur of appreciation rose again from the girls assembled.

"I do not recall at this moment just how much insurance was on the West Dormitory; I leave those details to Doctor Tellingham, and he is now looking up the papers in the office. But I am sure there is ample to rebuild, and if all goes well, a new West Dormitory will rise in the place of these smoking ruins before our patrons and our friends come to our graduation exercises in June."

"Oh, bully!" cried Ann Hicks, under her breath. "I want Uncle Bill to see Briarwood at its very best."

"But the dear old ivy never can be replaced," Mercy Curtis murmured to Ruth.

"We shall endeavor," went on Mrs. Tellingham, smiling, "to

repeat in the new building all the advantages of the old. We shall have everything replaced, if possible, exactly as it was before the fire."

"There was a big inkspot on my rug," muttered Jennie Stone. "Bet they can't get *that* just in the same place again."

"You homeless girls must, in the meanwhile, possess your souls with patience. The younger girls who had quarters in the West Dormitory will be made comfortable in the East. But you older girls must be cared for in a different way.

"Some few I shall take into my own apartments, or otherwise find room for in the main building here. Some, however, will have to occupy quarters outside the school premises until the new building is constructed and ready for occupancy. Arrangements for these quarters I have already made. And now we can separate for our usual classes and work, with the feeling that all will come out right and that the new dormitory will be built within reasonable time."

She ceased speaking. The door near the platform suddenly opened and "the old doctor" as the girls called the absent-minded husband of their preceptress, hastily entered.

He stumbled up to the platform, waving a number of papers in his hand. He stammered so that he could hardly speak at first, and he gave no attention to the amazed girls in the audience.

"Mrs. Tellingham! Mrs. Tellingham!" he ejaculated. "I have made a great mistake—an unpardonable error! In renewing the insurance for the various buildings I overlooked that for the West Dormitory and its contents. The insurance on that ran out a week ago. There was not a dollar on it when it burned last night!"

CHAPTER XII

"GREAT OAKS FROM LITTLE ACORNS GROW"

Mercy Curtis was one of the older girls quartered in Mrs. Tellingham's suite. She told her close friends how Doctor Tellingham walked the floor of the inner office and bemoaned his absent-mindedness that had brought disaster upon Mrs. Tellingham and the whole school.

"I know that Mrs. Tellingham is becoming more worried about the doctor than about the lapsed insurance," said Mercy. "Of course, he's a foolish old man without any more head than a pin! But why did she leave the business of renewing the insurance in his charge, in the first place?"

"Oh, Mercy!" protested Ruth.

"No more head than a pin!" repeated Nettie Parsons, in horror. "Why! who ever heard the like? He writes histories! He must be a very brainy man."

"Who ever *reads* them?" grumbled Mercy.

"They look awfully solid," confessed Lluella Fairfax. "Did you ever look at the whole row of them in the office bookcase?"

Jennie Stone began to giggle. "I don't care," she said, "the doctor may be a great historian; but his memory is just as short as it can be. Do you know what happened only last half when he and Mrs. Tellingham were invited to the Lumberton Association Ball?"

"What was it?" asked Helen.

"I suppose it is something perfectly ridiculous, or Heavy wouldn't have remembered it," Ruth suggested.

"Thank you!" returned the plump girl, making a face. "I have a better memory than Dr. Tellingham, I should hope."

"Come on! tell the joke, Heavy," urged Mary Cox.

"Why, when he came into the office ready to escort Mrs. Tellingham to the ball, Mrs. T. criticised his tie. 'Do go back, Doctor, and put on a black tie,' she said. You know, he's the best natured old dear in the world," Jennie pursued, "and he went right back into his bedroom to make the change. They waited, and they waited, and then they waited some more," chuckled Jennie. "The doctor did not reappear. So Mrs. Tellingham finally went to his bedroom and opened the door. She saw that the old doctor, having removed the tie she didn't like, had continued the process of undressing, and just as Mrs. Tellingham looked in, he climbed placidly into bed."

"I can believe that," said Ann Hicks, when the laughter had subsided.

"And I can believe that both he and Mrs. Tellingham are just as worried about the destruction of the dormitory as they can be," Nettie added. "All their money is invested in the school, is it not?"

"Except that invested in the doctor's useless histories," said Mercy, who was inclined to be most unmerciful of speech on occasion.

"Is there nobody to help them rebuild?" asked Ann, tentatively.

"Not a soul," declared Ruth.

"I believe I'll write to Uncle Bill Hicks. He'll help, I know," said Ann. "Next to Heavy's Aunt Kate, Uncle Bill thinks that the finest woman on this footstool is Mrs. Tellingham."

"And I'll ask papa for some money," Nettie said quickly. "I had that in mind from the first."

"My father will give some," Helen said.

"We'll write to Madge Steele," said Belle. "Her father might help, too."

"I guess all our folks will be willing to help," Lluella Fairfax added.

"And," said Jennie, "here's Ruth, with a fortune in her own right."

But Ruth did not make any rejoinder to Jennie's remark and that surprised them all; for they knew Ruth Fielding was not stingy.

"We are going about this thing in the wrong way, girls," she said quietly. "At least, I think we are."

"How are we?" demanded Helen. "Surely, we all want to help Mrs. Tellingham."

"And Old Briarwood," cried Belle Tingley.

"And all the students of our Alma Mater will want to join in," maintained Lluella.

"Now you've said it!" cried Ruth, with a sudden smile. "Every girl who is now attending the dear old Hall will want to help rebuild the West Dormitory."

"All can give their mites, can't they?" demanded Jennie. "And the rich can give of their plenty."

"That is just it," Ruth went on, still seriously. "Nettie's father will give a good sum; so will Helen's; so will Mr. William Hicks, who is one of the most liberal men in the world. Therefore, the little gifts of the other girls' parents will look terribly small."

"Oh, Ruth! don't say that our folks can't give," cried Jennie, whose father likewise was rich.

"It is not in my province to say who shall, or who shall not give," declared Ruth, hastily. "I only want to point out to you girls that if the rich give a great deal the poorer will almost be ashamed to give what they can."

"That's right," said Mary Cox, suddenly. "We haven't much; so we couldn't give much."

The girls looked rather troubled; but Ruth had not finished. "There is another thing," she said. "If all your fathers give to the dormitory fund, what will you girls personally give?"

"Oh! how's that, Ruth?" cried Helen.

"Say," drawled Jennie Stone, the plump girl, "we're not all

Alice B. Emerson

fixed like you, Ruth—with a bank account to draw on."

Ruth blushed; but she did not lose her temper. "You don't understand what I mean yet," she said. "Either I am particularly muddy in my suggestions, or you girls are awfully dense to-day."

"How polite! how polite!" murmured Jennie.

"What I am trying to get at," Ruth continued earnestly, "is the fact that the rebuilding of the West Dormitory should interest us girls more than anybody else in the world, save Mrs. Tellingham."

"Well—doesn't it?" demanded Mary Cox, rather sharply.

"Does it interest us all enough for each girl to be willing to do something personally, or sacrifice something, toward the new building?" asked Ruth.

"I getcha, Steve!" exclaimed the slangy Jennie.

"Oh, dear me, Ruthie! we *are* dense," said Nettie. "Of course! every girl should be able to do as much as the next one. Otherwise there may be hard feelings."

"Secret heartburnings," added Helen.

"Of course," Mercy said, "Ruth would see *that* side of it. I don't expect my folks could give ten dollars toward the fund; but I should want to do as much as any girl here. Nobody loves Briarwood Hall more than I do," added the lame girl, fiercely.

"I believe you, dear," Ruth said. "And what we want to do is to invent some way of earning money in which every girl will have her part, and do her part, and feel that she has done her full share in rebuilding the West Dormitory."

"Hurrah!" cried Jennie. "That's the talk! I tell you, Ruth, you are the only bright girl in this school!"

"Thank you," said Ruth. "You cannot flatter me into believing that."

"But what's the idea, dear?" demanded Helen, eagerly. "You have some nice invention, I am sure. You always do have."

"Another base flatterer!" cried Ruth, laughing gaily. "I believe you girls say such things just to jolly me along, and so that you will not have to exercise any gray matter yourselves."

"Oh! oh!" groaned Jennie. "How ungrateful."

"Of course you have something to suggest?" Nettie said.

"No, not a thing. My idea is, merely, that we start something that every girl in the school can have her share in. Of course, that does not cut out contributions from those who have money to spare; but the new building must be erected by the efforts of the girls of Briarwood Hall as—"

"As a bunch of briars," chuckled Jennie. "Isn't that a sharp one?"

"Just as sharp as you are, my dear," said Helen.

"You know what that means, Heavy," said Mary Cox. "You're all curves."

"Oh! ouch! I know that hurt me," declared the plump girl,

altogether too good-natured to be offended by anything her mates said to her.

"So that's how it is," Ruth finished "Call the girls together. Put the idea before them. Let's hear from everybody, and see which girl has the best thought along this line. We want a way of making money in which everyone can join."

"I—don't—see," complained Nettie, "how you are going to do it."

"Never mind. Don't worry," said Mercy. "'Great oaks from little acorns grow,' and a fine idea will sprout from the germ of Ruth's suggestion, I have no doubt."

It did; but not at all in the way any of them expected. The whole school was called together after recitations on this afternoon, which was several days following the fire. The teachers had no part in the assembly, least of all Mrs. Tellingham.

But the older girls—all of them S.B.'s—were very much in earnest; and from them the younger pupils, of course, took their cue. The West Dormitory must be built—and within the time originally specified by Mrs. Tellingham when she had thought the insurance would fully pay for the work of reconstruction.

Many girls, it seemed, had already written home begging contributions to the fund which they expected would be raised for the new building. Some even were ready to offer money of their very own toward the amount necessary to start the work.

Even Ruth agreed to this first effort to get money. She pledged a hundred dollars herself and Nettie Parsons quietly put down the same sum as her own personal offering.

"Oh, gracious, goodness, me, girls!" gasped Jennie Stone, who had been figuring desperately upon a sheet of paper. "Wait till I get this sum done; then I can tell you what I will give. There! Can it be possible?"

"What is it, Jennie?" asked Belle Tingley, looking over her shoulder. "Why! look at all those figures. Are you weighing the sun or counting the hairs of the sun-dogs?"

"Don't laugh," begged the plump girl. "This is a serious matter. I've been figuring up what I should probably have spent for candy from now till June if I'd been left to my own will."

"What is it, Heavy?" asked somebody. "I wager it would pay for erecting the new dormitory without the rest of us putting up a cent."

"No," said the plump girl, gravely. "But it figures up to a good round sum. I never would have believed it! Girls, I'll give fifty dollars."

"Oh, Heavy! you *never* could eat so much sweets before graduation," gasped one.

"I could; but I sha'n't," declared Miss Stone, with continued gravity. "I'll practise self-denial."

With all the fun and joking, the girls of Briarwood Hall were very much in earnest. They elected a committee of five— Ruth, Nettie, Lluella, Sarah Fish and Mary Cox—to have charge of the collection of the fund, and to go immediately to Mrs. Tellingham and show her what money was already promised and how much more could be expected within ten days.

There was enough, they knew, to warrant the preceptress in having the work of tearing away the ruins begun. Meanwhile, the girls were each urged to think up some new way of earning money, and as a committee of the whole to try to invent a novel scheme of including the whole school in a plan whereby much money might be raised.

"How we're to do it, nobody knows," said Helen gloomily, walking along beside Ruth after the meeting. "I expected *you* would have just the thing to suggest."

"I wish I had," her chum returned thoughtfully.

"Mercy says, 'Great oaks from little acorns grow'—"

They turned into the hall and saw that the mail had been distributed. Ruth was handed a letter with Mr. Hammond's name upon it. She had almost forgotten the moving picture man and her own scenario, in these three or four very busy days.

Ruth eagerly tore the envelope open. A green slip of paper fluttered out. It was a check for twenty-five dollars from the Alectrion Film Corporation. With it was a note highly praising Ruth's first effort at scenario writing for moving pictures.

"What is it?" demanded Helen. "You look so funny. There's no—nobody dead?"

"Do I look like that?" asked Ruth. "Far from it! Just look at these, dear," and she thrust both the note and the check into Helen's hands. "I believe I've struck it!"

"Struck what?" demanded her puzzled chum.

"'Great oaks from little acorns grow' sure enough! Eureka! I have it," Ruth cried. "I believe I know how we all—every girl in Briarwood—can help earn the money to rebuild the West Dormitory."

Alice B. Emerson

CHAPTER XIII

THE IDEA IS BORN

"What? What? *What*?" Helen cried, as she gazed, wide-eyed, at the check and at Mr. Hammond's letter.

The check for twenty-five dollars there could be no mistake about; and she scanned the moving picture man's enthusiastic letter shortly, for it was brief. But Helen quite misunderstood the well-spring of Ruth's sudden joy.

"Oh, Ruthie Fielding!" she gasped. "What have you done now?" and she hugged her chum delightedly. "How wonderful! *that* was the secret between you and that Mr. Hammond, was it?"

"Yes," admitted Ruth.

"And you've written a *real* moving picture?"

"That is it—exactly. A *one* reel picture," and Ruth laughed.

"And he says he will produce it at once," sighed Helen.

"So Mr. Hammond says. It's very nice of him."

"Oh, Ruth!" cried Helen, hugging her again.

"Oh, Helen!" responded Ruth, in sheer delight.

"You're famous—really famous!" said Ruth's chum, with sudden solemnity.

Ruth's clear laughter rang out spontaneously.

"Well, you are!"

"Not yet."

"But you've earned twenty-five dollars writing that play. Only think of that! And you can give it to the dormitory fund. Is that what you are so pleased about? Mercy, Ruth! you don't expect us all to set about writing picture plays and selling them to Mr. Hammond?"

"No," said Ruth, more seriously. "I guess that wouldn't do."

"Then what do you mean about every girl at Briarwood helping in this way toward the fund?" Helen asked, puzzled. "At any rate, twenty-five dollars will help."

"But I sha'n't do that!" cried Ruth.

"Sha'n't do what?"

"I shall not give this precious twenty-five dollars to any dormitory fund—no, indeed!" and Ruth clasped the check to her bosom. "The first money I ever earned with my pen? I guess not! That twenty-five dollars goes into the bank, my dear."

"Goodness! You needn't be so emphatic about it," protested Helen.

"I am going to open a special account," said Ruth, proudly. "This will be credited to the fact that R.F. can actually make something *with her brains*, my lady. What do you think?"

"But how is it going to help the dormitory fund, then?" demanded her chum.

"Not by adding my poor little twenty-five dollars to it. We want hundreds—*thousands*! Don't you understand, Helen, that my check would only be a drop in the bucket? And, anyway, I would come near to starving before I would use this check."

"We—ell! I don't know that I blame you," sighed her friend. "I'd be as pleased as Punch if it were mine. Just think of your writing a real moving picture!" she repeated. "Won't the girls be surprised? And suppose it comes to Lumberton and we can all go and see it? You *will* be famous, Ruth."

"I don't know about that, dear," Ruth returned happily. "There is something about it all that you don't see yet."

"What's that?"

"This success of mine, I tell you, has given me a great, big idea."

"About what?"

"For the dormitory fund," Ruth said. "Mercy is right. Great oaks *do* grow from little acorns."

"Who's denying it?" demanded Helen. "Go on."

"Out of this little idea of mine which I have sold to Mr. Hammond, comes a thought, dear," said Ruth, solemnly, "that may get us all the money we need to rebuild the West Dormitory."

"I—don't—just—see—"

"But you will," cried Ruth. "Let me explain. If I can write a one-reel picture play, why not a long one—a real play—a five-reel drama? I have just the idea for it—oh, a grand idea!"

"Oh, Ruth!" murmured Helen, clasping her hands.

"I will write the play, we will all act in it, and Mr. Hammond shall produce it. It can be shown around in every city and town from which we girls come—our home towns, you know. Folks will want to see us Briarwood girls acting for the movies—won't they?"

"I should say they would! Fancy our doing that?"

"We can do it. Of course we can! And we'll get a royalty from the film and that will all go into the dormitory fund," went on the enthusiastic Ruth.

"Oh, my dear!" gasped Helen. "Would Mr. Hammond take such a play if you wrote it?"

"Of course I don't know. If not he, then some other producer. I *know* I have a novel idea," asserted Ruth.

"What is it?" asked the curious Helen.

"A schoolgirl picture, just as I say. Of course, there will have to be some *real* actors in it; we girls couldn't be funny enough, or serious enough, perhaps, to take the most important parts. We could act out some real scenes of boarding

Alice B. Emerson

school life, just the same."

"I should say we could!" cried Helen. "Who better? Stage one of our old midnight sprees, and show Heavy gobbling everything in sight. That would make 'em laugh."

"But we want more than a comedy," Ruth said seriously. "I have the germ of an idea in my mind. I'll write Mr. Hammond about it first of all. And we must have Miss Gray in it."

"He says here," said Helen, glancing through the moving picture man's letter again, "that he wants you to try another. Oh! and he says that in a few days he is coming to Lumberton with a company to take some films."

"So he does! Oh, goody!" cried Ruth. "I'll see him, then, and talk right to him. He is an awfully rich man—so Hazel Gray told me. We'll get him interested in the dormitory fund, anyway, and then, whether I can write a five-reel drama well enough or not, maybe he can find somebody who will put it into shape," Ruth added.

"Why, my dear!" exclaimed her chum, with scorn. "If you have written *one* moving picture, of course you can another."

Which did not follow at all, Ruth was sure.

"We'll have to ask Mrs. Tellingham," said Helen, with sudden doubt. "Maybe she will not approve."

"Oh! I hope she will," cried Ruth. "But we must put it up to the girls themselves, first of all. They must all be in it. All must have an interest—all must take part. Otherwise it will not accomplish the end we are after."

"Oh, oh, oh!" cried Helen, finally waking up. "Of course! this is the very thing you wanted, Ruthie—to give every girl something to do that is important toward earning the money for the building of the new dormitory."

"That's it, my dear. We all must appear, and do our part. School scenes, recreation scenes, athletic scenes in the gym; marching in our graduation procession; initiating candidates into the S.B. sorority; Old Noah's Ark with the infants arriving at the beginning of the year; the dance we always have in the big hall at holiday time—just a great, big picture of what boarding school girls do, and how they live, breathe and have their being!"

"Oh, jolly!" gasped Helen, taking fire from her friend's enthusiasm. "Say! the girls are going to be just about crazy over this, Ruth. You will be the most popular girl in the school."

"I hope not!" gasped Ruth, in real panic. "I'm not doing this for any such purpose. Don't be singing my praises all the time, Helen. The girls will get sick and tired to death of hearing about 'wonderful me.' We all want to do something to help Mrs. Tellingham and the school. That's all there is to it. Now, *do* be sensible."

They were not long in taking the girls at large into their confidence. When it was known that Ruth Fielding had actually written one scenario for a film, which had been accepted, paid for, and would be produced, naturally the enthusiasm over the idea of having a reproduction of school life at Briarwood filmed, became much greater than it might otherwise have been. As a whole, the girls of Briarwood Hall were in a mood to work together for the fund.

"No misunderstandings," said Jennie Stone, firmly. "We don't want to make the sort of mistake the rural constable did when he came along by the riverside and saw a face floating on the water. 'Come out o' that!' he says. 'You know there ain't no bathing allowed around here.' And the face in the water answered: 'Excuse me, officer; I'm not bathing—I'm only drowning!'"

"We've all got to pull together," the plump girl continued, very much in earnest. "No hanging back—no squabbling over little things. If Ruth Fielding can write a picture play we must all do our prettiest in acting in it. Why! I'd play understudy to a baby elephant in a circus for the sake of helping build the new dormitory."

Already Mrs. Tellingham and the doctor had been informed by the girls' executive committee of the sums both actually raised by the girls, and promised, toward the dormitory fund. It had warranted the good lady's signing contracts for the removal of the wreckage of the burned building, at least. The way would soon be cleared for beginning work on a new structure.

Offers of money came pouring in from the parents interested in the success of Briarwood Hall; and some of the checks already received by Mrs. Tellingham were for substantial sums. But this proposal of Ruth's for all the girls to help in the increase of the fund, pleased Mrs. Tellingham more than anything else.

She read Ruth's brief sketch of the plot she had originated for the school play, and approved it. "The Heart of a Schoolgirl" was forthwith put into shape to show Mr. Hammond when he came to Lumberton, that event being expected daily.

About this time the girls of Briarwood Hall were so excited and interested over the moving picture idea that they scarcely had time for their studies and usual work.

CHAPTER XIV

AT MRS. SADOC SMITH'S

Mrs Tellingham, wise in the ways of girls, had foreseen the excitement and disturbance in the placid current of Briarwood life, and made plans following the fire to counteract the evil influences of just this disturbance. The girls who hoped to graduate from the school in the coming June must have more quiet—must have time to study and to think.

The younger girls, if they fell behind in their work, could make it up in the coming terms. Not so Ruth Fielding and her friends, so the wise school principal had distributed them, after the destruction of the West Dormitory, in such manner that they would be free from the hurly-burly of the general school life.

A few, like Mercy Curtis (who could not easily walk back and forth from any outside lodging), Mrs. Tellingham kept in her own apartment. But the greater number of the graduating class was distributed among neighbors who—in most cases—were not averse to accepting good pay for rooms which could only be let to summer boarders and were, at this time of year, never occupied.

The Briarwood Hall preceptress allowed her girls to go only

Alice B. Emerson

where she could trust the land-ladies to have some oversight over their lodgers. And the girls themselves were bound in honor to obey the rules of the school, whether on the Briarwood premises or not.

Visiting among the outside scholars was forbidden, and the girls studying for graduation had their hours more to themselves than they would have had in the school.

Special chums were able to keep together in most instances. Ruth, Helen and Ann Hicks went to live at Mrs. Sadoc Smith's; and there was room in the huge front room on the second floor of her rambling old house, for Mercy, too, had it been wise for the lame girl to lodge so far from the school.

Mrs. Smith got the girls up in season in the morning to reach the dining hall at Briarwood by breakfast-time; and she saw to it, likewise, that their light went out at ten o'clock in the evening. These were her instructions from Mrs. Tellingham, and Mrs. Sadoc Smith was rather a grim person, who did her duty and obeyed the law.

There being an extra couch, Ruth persuaded her friends to agree to the coming of a fourth girl into the lodging. And this fourth girl, oddly enough, was not one of the graduating class, or even one of the girls whom they had chummed with before.

It was the new girl, Amy Gregg! Amy Gregg, whom nobody seemed to want, and who seemed to be the loneliest figure and the most sullen girl who had ever come to Briarwood Hall!

"Of course, you'd pick up some sore-eyed kitten," complained Ann Hicks. "That child has a fully-developed grouch against the whole world, I verily believe. What do you want her for, Ruthie?"

"I don't want her," said Ruth promptly.

"Well! of all the girls!" gasped Helen. "Then *why* ask Mrs. Tellingham to let her come here?"

"Because she ought to be with somebody who will look out for her," Ruth said.

She did not tell her mates about it, but Ruth had heard some whispers regarding the origin of the fire that had burned down the West Dormitory, and she was afraid Amy would be suspected.

The older girl had reason to know that Mrs. Tellingham had questioned Amy regarding the candle she had obtained from Miss Scrimp's store. The girl had emphatically denied having left the candle burning on leaving her room to go to supper on the fatal evening.

The girls had begun, after a time, to ask questions about the origin of the fire. They knew it had started on the side of the corridor where Amy Gregg had roomed. They might soon suspect the truth.

"If they do, good-bye to all little Gregg's peace of mind!" Ruth thought, for she knew just how cruel girls can be, and Amy did not readily make friends.

Although Ruth and her room-mates tried to make the flaxen-haired girl feel at home at Mrs. Sadoc Smith's, Amy remained sullen, and seemed afraid of the older girls. She was particularly unpopular, too, because she was the only girl who had refused to write home to tell of the fire and ask for a contribution to the dormitory fund.

Alice B. Emerson

Amy Gregg seemed to be afraid to talk of the fire and refused to give even a dollar toward the rebuilding of the dormitory. "It isn't *my* fault that the old thing burned down. I lost all my clothes and books," she announced. "I think the school ought to pay *me* some money, instead."

After saying this before her room-mates at Mrs. Smith's, all but Ruth dropped her.

"Sullen little thing," said Helen, with disgust.

"Not worth bothering with," rejoined Ann.

The only person to whom Amy Gregg seemed to take a fancy was Mrs. Smith's scapegrace grandson, Henry. Henry was the wildest boy there was anywhere about Briarwood Hall. He was always getting into trouble, and his grandmother was forever chastising him in one way or another.

Nobody in the neighborhood knew him as "Henry." He was called "that Smith boy" by the grown folk; by his mates he was known as "Curly."

Ruth felt that Curly never would have developed into such a mischievous and wayward youth had it not been for his grandmother.

When a little boy Henry had come to live with Mrs. Sadoc Smith. Mrs. Smith did not like boys and she kept Henry in kilts until he was of an age when most lads are looking forward to long trousers. She made him wear Fauntleroy suits and kept his hair in curls down his back—molasses colored curls that disgusted the boy mightily. Finally he hired another boy for ten cents and a glass agate to cut the curls off close to his head, and he stole a pair of long trousers, a world too wide for him, from a neighbor's line. He then set out on his travels, going in an empty freight car from the Lumberton railroad yards.

But he was caught and brought back, literally "by the scruff of his neck;" and his grandmother was never ending in her talk about the escapade. The curls remained short, however. If she refused to give Curly twenty cents occasionally to have his hair cut, he would stick burrs or molasses taffy in the hair so that it had to be kept short.

There seemed an affinity between this scapegrace lad and Amy Gregg. Not that she possessed any abundance of spirit; but she would listen to Curly romance about his adventures by the hour, and he could safely confide all his secrets to Amy Gregg. Wild horses would not have drawn a word from her as to his intentions, or what mischief he had already done.

Curly was a tall, thin boy of fifteen, wiry and strong, and with a face as smooth and pink-and-white as a girl's. That he was so girlish looking was a sore subject with the boy, and whenever any unwise boy called him "Girly" instead of "Curly" it started a fight, there and then.

Henry was forbidden by his grandmother to bother the girls from Briarwood Hall in any way, and to make sure that he played no tricks upon them, when Ruth and her mates came to the house to lodge, Mrs. Smith housed Curly in a little, steep-roofed room over the summer kitchen.

It was a cold and uncomfortable place, he told Amy Gregg. Ruth heard him tell her so, but judged that it would not be wise to beg Mrs. Smith for other quarters for her grandson. She was not a woman to whom one could easily give advice—especially one of Ruth's age and inexperience.

Alice B. Emerson

Mrs. Smith was a very grim looking woman with a false front of little, corkscrew curls, the color of which did not at all match the iron-gray of her hair. That the curls were made of Mrs. Smith's own hair, cropped from her head many years before, there could be no doubt. It Nature had erred in turning her actual hair to iron-gray in these, her later years, that was Nature's fault, not Mrs. Smith's!

She grimly ignored the parti-colored hair as she did the natural exuberance of her grandson's spirit. If Nature had given him an unquenchable amount of mirth and jollity, that, too, was Nature's fault. Still, Mrs. Sadoc Smith proposed to quell that mirth and suppress the joy of Curly's nature if possible.

The only question was: In the process of making Curly over to fit her ideas of what a boy should be, was not Mrs. Smith running a grave chance of ruining the boy entirely?

And what boy, living in a house with four girls, could keep from trying to play tricks upon them? If the shed-chamber had been a mile away over the roofs of the Smith house, Curly would have been tempted to creep over the shingles to one of the windows of the big front room, and—

Nine o'clock at night. All four of the girls quartered with Mrs. Smith were busy with their books—even flaxen-haired Amy Gregg. The rustle of turning leaves and a sigh of weariness now and then was all that had broken the silence for half an hour.

Outside, the wind moaned in the trees. It was cold and the sky was overcast with the promise of a stormy morrow. Suddenly Helen started and glanced hastily at the window behind her, where the shade was drawn.

"What's that?" she whispered.

"Huh?" said Ann.

"I didn't hear anything," Ruth added.

Not a word from Amy Gregg, who likewise appeared to be deeply immersed in her book.

Another silence; then both Ruth and Helen jumped. "I declare! Is that a bird or a beast?" Helen demanded.

"What is it?" cried Ann, starting up.

"Somebody rapping on that window," Ruth declared.

"This far up from the ground? Nonsense!" exclaimed the bold Ann, and marched to the casement and ran up the shade.

They could see nothing. There was no light in the roadway before the house. Ann opened the window and leaned out.

"Nobody down there throwing up gravel, that's sure," she declared, drawing in her head again, and shutting the window.

Just as they returned to their books the scratching, squeaking noise broke out again. This time Ruth ran to see.

"Nothing!" she confessed.

"What do you suppose it can be?" asked Helen nervously. "I declare, I can't study any more. That gets on my nerves."

Mrs. Smith put in her head at that moment. "Of course you haven't seen that boy, any of you?" she asked sharply.

The three older girls looked at each other; Amy Gregg continued to pore over her book. No; Ruth, Helen and Ann could honestly tell Mrs. Smith that they had not seen Curly.

"Well, the young rascal has slipped out. I went up to his door to take him some clothes I had mended, and he didn't answer. So I opened the door, and his bed hasn't been touched, and he went up an hour ago. He's slipped out over the shed roof, for his window's open; though I don't see how he dared drop to the ground. It's twenty feet if it's an inch," Mrs. Smith said sternly.

"I shall wait up for him and catch him when he comes back. I'll learn him to go out nights without me knowin' of it."

She went away, stepping wrathfully. "Goodness! I'm sorry for that boy," said Ann, beginning leisurely to prepare for bed.

But Ruth watched Amy Gregg curiously. She saw the smaller girl flush and pale and glance now and then toward the window. Ruth jumped to a sudden conclusion. Curly was somewhere outside that window on the roof!

CHAPTER XV

A DAWNING POSSIBILITY

"Well, the evening's spoiled anyway," yawned Helen, seeing Ann braiding her hair. "I might as well stop, too," and she closed her books with relief.

"It's time small girls were on their way to the Land of Nod," said the Western girl, taking the book from the resisting hand of Amy Gregg. "Hullo! it's time *you* were in bed, girlie, sure enough. Holding the book upside down, no less! What do you know about that, ladies?"

"Certainly she should go to bed," Helen said sharply. "We're all sleepy. Do hurry, child."

"Speak for yourself, Helen," snapped Amy. "I don't have to mind *you*, I hope."

"You do if you want to get anywhere in this school—and mind every other senior who is kind enough to notice you," said Ann. "You've not learned that lesson yet."

"And I don't believe *you* can teach me," responded the younger girl, ready to quarrel with anybody. "Give me back my book!"

Ruth went to her and put her arm around Amy's neck. "Don't, dear, be so fractious," she begged. "We had all to go through a process of 'fagging' when we first came to Briarwood. It is good for us—part of the discipline. I asked Mrs. Tellingham to let you come over here with us so that you really would not be put upon—"

"I don't thank you!" snapped Amy, ungratefully. "I can look out for myself, I guess. I always have."

"You're like the self-made man," drawled Ann. "You've made an awfully poor job of it! You need a little discipline, my dear."

"Not from you!" cried the other girl, her eyes flashing.

It took Ruth several minutes to quiet this sea of trouble. It was half an hour before Amy cried herself to sleep on her couch. The other girls had both crept into bed and called to Ruth sleepily to put out the light. Ruth was not undressed; but she did as they requested.

Then she went to the window and opened it. Nothing had been heard from above since Mrs. Smith had looked in at the chamber door. But Ruth was sure the grim old woman was waiting at her grandson's window, in the cold shed bedroom, ready for Curly when he came in.

And Ruth was sure, too, that the boy had not dropped to the ground. *He was still on the roof.*

"That was a tictac," Ruth told herself. She had heard Tom Cameron's too many times to mistake the sound. "And Amy was expecting it. Curly had told her what he was going to do. And now what will that reckless boy do, with his grandmother waiting for him and every other window in the house locked?"

"What are you doing there, Ruthie?" grumbled Ann. "O-o-oh! it's cold," and she drew her comforter up around her shoulders and the next moment she was asleep.

Helen never lay awake after her head touched the pillow, so Ruth did not look for any questioning on her chum's part. And Amy had already wept herself unhappily into dreamland.

"Poor kiddie!" thought Ruth, casting a commiserating glance again at Amy. "And now for this silly boy. If the girls knew what I was going to do they'd have a spasm, I expect," and she chuckled.

She leaned far out of the open window again, and, sitting on the window-sill, turned her body so as to look up the slant of the steep roof.

"Curly!" she called softly. No answer. "Curly Smith!" she raised her voice decisively. "If you don't come here I'll call your grandmother."

A figure appeared slowly from behind a chimney. Even at that distance Ruth could see the figure shiver.

"Wha—what do you want?" asked the boy, shakingly.

"Come here, you silly boy!" commanded Ruth. "Do you want to get your death of cold?"

"I—I—"

"Come down here at once! And don't fall, for pity's sake," was Ruth's warning, as the boy's foot slipped. "My goodness!

you haven't any shoes on—and no cap—and just that thin coat. Curly Smith! you'll be down sick after this."

"I'll be sick if Gran' catches me," admitted the boy. "She's layin' for me at my window."

"I know," said Ruth, as the boy crept closer.

"You telltale girls told her, of course," growled the boy.

"We did not. Ann and Helen don't know. Amy is scared, but she's gone to sleep. *She* wouldn't tell."

"How did Gran' know, then?" demanded Curly, coming closer.

Ruth told him. The boy was both ashamed of his predicament and frightened.

"How can I get in, Ruth? I'd like to sneak downstairs into the sitting room and lie down by the sitting room fire and get warm."

"You shall. Come in this way," commanded Ruth. "But, for pity's sake, don't fall!"

"She'll find it out and lick me worse," said Curly, doubtfully.

"She won't. The girls are asleep, I tell you."

"Well, *you* know it, don't you?" demanded Curly, with desperation.

"Curly Smith! If you think I'd tell on you, you deserve to stay out here on this roof and freeze," declared Ruth, in anger.

"Oh, say! don't get mad," said Curly, fearing that she would leave him as she intimated.

"Come on, then—and whisper. Not a sound when you get in the room. And for pity's sake, Curly Smith—don't fall!"

"Not going to," growled the boy. "Look out and let me swing down to that window-sill. Ugh! I 'most slipped then. Look out!"

Ruth wriggled back into the room and almost immediately Curly's unshod feet appeared on the sill. She grasped his ankles firmly.

"Come in!" she whispered. "That's the boy! Quick, now!"

All this in low whispers. The girls did not stir, and Ruth had no light. She could barely see the figure of the boy between her and the gray light out-of-doors.

Curly dropped softly into the room. Ruth led him by the hand to the door, which she opened softly. The hall was pitch dark, too.

"You're all right, Ruthie Fielding!" he muttered, as he passed her and stepped into the hall. "I won't forget this."

Ruth thought it might be a warning to him. In the morning his grandmother admitted having found the boy curled up in a rug and asleep before the sitting-room fire.

"An' I thought he was out o' doors all the time," she said. "I ought to punish him, anyway, I s'pose, for scaring me so."

Ruth Fielding spent all her spare time (and that was not much, for her studies were just then very engrossing) in planning and sketching out the five-reel drama in which she hoped to interest Mr. Hammond, head of the Alectrion Film Corporation. She called up the Lumberton Hotel every day to learn if the film company had arrived.

At length the clerk told her Mr. Hammond himself had come, and expected his company the next day. Mr. Hammond was near and was soon speaking to the girl of the Red Mill over the telephone.

"Is this the famous authoress of 'Curiosity?'" asked Mr. Hammond, laughing. "I have received your signed contract and acceptance, and the scenario is already in rehearsal. I hope everything is perfectly satisfactory, Miss Fielding?"

"Oh, Mr. Hammond! I'm not joking. I want to see you very, very much."

"About 'Curiosity?'"

"Oh, no, sir! I'm very grateful to you for taking that and paying me for it, as I told you," Ruth said. "But this is something different—and much more important. *When* can I see you?"

"Any time after breakfast and before bedtime, my dear," Mr. Hammond assured her. "Do you want to come to town, or shall I come to Briarwood Hall?"

"If you would come here you could see Mrs. Tellingham, too, and that would be lots better," Ruth assured him.

"The principal of your school?" he asked, in surprise.

"Yes, Mr. Hammond. One of our buildings has burned down—"

"Oh! I saw that in the paper," interposed the gentleman. "It is too bad."

"It is tragic!" declared Ruth, earnestly. "There was no insurance, and all us girls want to help build a new dormitory. I have a plan—and *you* can help—"

"We—ell," said Mr. Hammond, doubtfully. "How much does this mean?"

"I don't know. If the idea is as good as I think it is, Mr. Hammond," Ruth told him, placidly, "you will make a lot of money, and so will Briarwood Hall."

"Hullo!" ejaculated the gentleman. "You expect to show me how to make some money? I thought you wanted a contribution."

"No. It is a bona fide scheme for making money," laughed Ruth. "Do run out sometime to-day and let me talk you into it. You shall meet Mrs. Tellingham, too."

The gentleman promised, and kept the promise promptly. He heard Ruth's idea, approved of it with enthusiasm, and went over with her the briefly outlined sketch for "The Heart of a Schoolgirl." He was able to suggest a number of important changes in Ruth's plan, and his ideas were all helpful and put with tact. Mr. Hammond and Mrs. Tellingham came to an understanding and made a written agreement, too.

Many of the pictures were to be taken at Briarwood Hall. Mrs. Tellingham, on behalf of the dormitory fund, was to have a certain interest in the profits of the production. These legal and technical matters Ruth had nothing to do with. She was able, with an untrammeled mind, to go on with the actual work of writing the scenario.

CHAPTER XVI

THE CAT OUT OF THE BAG

Those were really strenuous days indeed for Ruth Fielding and her friends at Briarwood Hall. The class that looked forward to graduating in June was exceedingly busy.

Had Mrs. Tellingham not made an equitable arrangement in regard to Ruth's English studies, allowing her credits on her writing, the girl of the Red Mill would never have found time for the writing of the scenario which all hoped would ultimately bring a large sum into the dormitory fund.

With faith in her pupil's ability as a writer for the screen, Mrs. Tellingham had gone on with the work of clearing away the ruins of the burned building, and had given out contracts for the construction of the new dormitory on the site of the old one.

The sums already gathered from voluntary contributions paid the bills as the work went along; but in "The Heart of a Schoolgirl" must lie the earning power to carry the work to completion.

As each girl of the senior class had special work in English of an original nature, Mrs. Tellingham announced that Ruth's scenario should count as her special thesis.

"We will let Mr. Hammond judge it, my dear," the principal said to Ruth. She was already proud of the girl's achievement in writing "Curiosity," for she had now read that first scenario. "If Mr. Hammond declares that your drama is worthy of production, you shall be marked 'perfect' in your original English work. That, I am sure, is fair."

In spite of all the studying she had to do, and her work on the scenario of the five-reel drama, Ruth found time to look after Amy Gregg. Not that the latter thanked her—far from it! Ruth, however, did what she thought to be her duty toward the younger girl.

Once Jennie Stone hinted that she suspected Amy of starting the dormitory fire, but Ruth stopped her with:

"Be careful what you say, Jennie Stone. I am sure you would not want to set the other girls against little Gregg. She's apt to have a hard time enough here at Briarwood, at best."

"Her own fault," declared the plump girl.

"Her unfortunate nature, I grant you," said Ruth, shaking her head. "But don't say anything to make it worse. You'd be sorry, you know."

"Huh! If she deserves to have it known that the fire started in her room—"

"But you don't know that!" again interrupted Ruth. "And if it chanced to be so, that's all the more reason why you should not suggest it to the other girls."

"Goodness, Ruth! you are so funny."

Alice B. Emerson

"Then laugh at me," responded Ruth, smiling. "I don't mind."

"Pshaw!" said Jennie. "There's no getting ahead of you. You're just like the little kid I heard of who was entertaining some other little girls at a nursery tea. 'My little sister is only five months old,' says one little girl, 'and she has two teeth.'"

"'My little sister is only six months old,' spoke up another guest, 'and she's got three teeth.'"

"The other kiddie was silent for a moment; she wanted to be polite, but she couldn't let the others put it over her like that! So finally she bursts out with:

"'Well, my little sister hasn't any teef yet; but when she *does* have some, they're goin' to be gold ones!' Couldn't get ahead of her—and nobody can get the best of *you*, Ruthie Fielding! You've always an answer ready."

At Mrs. Sadoc Smith's, Amy Gregg had just as little to do with the three older girls as she possibly could; but she remained friends with Curly. She was his confidant, and although Curly considered Ruth about the finest girl "who ever walked down the pike," as he expressed it, he felt in no awe of Amy Gregg and treated her more as he would another boy.

All was not plain sailing for Ruth in either her studies or in the writing of the scenario for "The Heart of a Schoolgirl." The coming examinations in all branches would be difficult, and unless she obtained a certain average in all, Ruth could not expect a diploma.

A diploma from Briarwood Hall was an entrance certificate to the college in which she and Helen hoped to continue their education the following autumn. And Ruth did not want to spend her summer in making up conditions. She wished to graduate in her class with a high grade.

It was a foregone conclusion in her mind that Mercy Curtis was to bear off the highest honor. Nor had she forgotten that she must invent (if nobody else could) a way for Mercy to speak the principal oration on graduation day.

Her powers of invention, however, were taxed to their utmost just now as she wrote the scenario of the picture drama. Before Mr. Hammond and the Alectrion Company left Lumberton, Ruth was able to get into town with the draft of the first part of the play, and read it to Mr. Hammond.

Miss Hazel Gray was present at the reading, and Ruth had given that pretty young girl a very good part indeed in the new film.

"You *dear*!" whispered Hazel, her arms around Ruth, and speaking to her softly, "I believe I have you to thank for much further consideration from Mr. Hammond. And you have given me a delightful part in this play you are writing. What a really wonderful child you are Ruth Fielding!"

Ruth thought that she was scarcely a child. But she only said: "I am glad you like the part. I meant it for you."

"I know. Mr. Hammond told me that you insisted on my playing the part of Eve Adair. And, oh! what about that nice boy, Thomas Cameron? Are he and his sister well? I received a lovely box of sweets from Thomas after I went back to the city that time."

"He is well, I believe," said Ruth, gravely. "He is not far from here, you know; he attends the Seven Oaks Military Academy."

Alice B. Emerson

"Oh! so he does. Maybe we shall go that way," said Hazel Gray, carelessly. "It would be lots of fun to see him again. Give my love to his sister."

"Yes, Miss Gray," Ruth returned seriously. "I will tell Helen."

She really liked Hazel Gray, and wished to see her get ahead. And it was through her acquaintanceship with Hazel that Ruth had made a friend of Mr. Hammond. But it annoyed Ruth that the actress should continue to be so friendly with Tom Cameron.

She thought no good could come of it Tom Cameron had always seemed such a seriously inclined boy, in spite of his ready fun and cheerfulness. To have him show such partiality for a girl so much older than himself, really a grown woman, as Hazel Gray was, disturbed Ruth.

She said nothing to her chum about it. If Helen was not worried about her twin's predilection for the moving picture actress, it did not become Ruth to worry.

Ruth went back to Briarwood, encouraged to go on with the writing of the drama. From Mr. Hammond's fertile mind had come several helpful suggestions. The plot of the play was very intimately connected with the history of Briarwood. There was included in its scenes a "Masque of the Marble Harp," in which the whole school was to be grouped about the fountain in the sunken garden.

The marble figure of Harmony, or Poesy, or whatever it was supposed to represent, was to come to life in the picture and strum the strings of the lyre which it held. This was a trick picture and Mr. Hammond had explained to Ruth just how it was to be made.

The legend of the marble harp, which had been kept alive by succeeding classes of Briarwood girls for the purpose of hazing "infants," came in very nicely now in Ruth's story. And the arrangement of this trick picture suggested another thing to Ruth Fielding, something which she had been racking her brains about for some time.

This idea had nothing to do with the present play; it had to do, instead, with Mercy Curtis and the graduation exercises. One idea bred another in Ruth Fielding's teeming brain. Her dramatic faculties, were being sharpened.

With all their regular studies and recitations, the seniors had to take their usual turns as monitors, and Ruth could not escape this duty. Besides, it was an honor not to be scorned, to be chosen to preside over the "primes," or to take the head of a table at dinner.

A teacher was ill on one day and Miss Brokaw asked Ruth to take certain classes of the primary grade. The recitations were on subjects quite familiar to Ruth and she felt no hesitancy in accepting the responsibility; but there was more ahead of her than she supposed when she entered on the task.

As it chanced, the flaxen-haired Amy Gregg was in the class of which Ruth was sent to take charge. Amy scowled at the senior when the latter took the desk; but most of the other girls were glad to see Ruth Fielding.

A little wrangle seemed to have begun before Ruth arrived, and the senior thought to settle the difficulty and start the day with "clear decks," by getting at the seat of the trouble.

"What is the matter, Mary Pease?" she asked a flushed and indignant girl who was angrily glaring at another. "Calm down, honey. Don't let your anger rise."

Alice B. Emerson

"If Amy Gregg says again that I took her gold pen, I'll tell something about *her* she won't like, now I warn her!" threatened Mary.

"Well, it's gone!" stormed Amy, "and you're the nearest. I'd like to know who took it if you didn't?"

"Well! of all the nerve! I want you to understand that I don't have to steal pens."

"Hold on, girls," put in Ruth. "This must not go on. You know, I shall be obliged to report you both."

"Of course!" snarled Amy. "You big girls are always telling on us."

"Oh!" and "Shame!" was the general murmur about the classroom; for most of the girls loved Ruth.

"Why, you nasty thing!" cried Mary Pease, glaring at Amy. "You ought to be ashamed. I'll tell what I know about *you*!"

"Mary!" exclaimed Ruth, with sudden fright. "Be still."

"I guess you don't know what I know about Gregg, Ruth Fielding," cried the excited Mary.

"We do not want to know," Ruth said hastily. "Let us stop this wrangling and turn to our work. Suppose Miss Brokaw should come in?"

"And I guess Miss Brokaw or anybody would want to know what I saw that night of the fire," declared Mary Pease, wildly. "*I* know whose room the fire started in, and *how* it started."

"Mary!" cried Ruth, rising from her seat, while the girls of the class uttered wondering exclamations.

But Mary was hysterical now.

"I saw a light in *her* room!" she cried, pointing an accusing finger at the white-faced and shaking Amy. "I peeped through the keyhole, and it was a candle burning on her table. She said she didn't have a candle. Bah!"

"Be still, Mary!" commanded Ruth again.

Amy Gregg was terror-stricken and shrank away from her accuser; but the latter was too excited to heed Ruth.

"I know all about it. So does Miss Scrimp. I told her. That Amy Gregg left the candle burning when she went to supper and it fell off her table into the waste basket.

"And that," concluded Mary Pease, "was how the fire started that burned down the West Dormitory, and I don't care who knows it, so there!"

CHAPTER XVII

ANOTHER OF CURLY'S TRICKS

Miss Scrimp, the matron of the old West Dormitory, had bound Mary Pease to secrecy. But, as Jennie put it, "the binding did not hold and *Pease* spilled the *beans*."

The story flew over the school like wildfire. Miss Scrimp, actually in tears, was inclined to blame Ruth Fielding for the outbreak of the story.

"You ought to have taken Mary Pease and run her right into a closet!" declared the matron. "Such behavior!"

Ruth was a good deal chagrined that the story should have come out while she was monitor; but she really did not see how she could have helped it. The quarrel between Amy Gregg and Mary Pease had commenced before Ruth had gone into the classroom.

"And how could you help it?" cried the faithful Jennie. "I expect little Pease has been aching to tell all these weeks. She should have been quarantined, in the first place."

But there was nothing to do about it now, save "to pick up the pieces." And that was no light task. Feeling ran high in

Briarwood Hall against Amy Gregg.

Some of the girls of her own age would not speak to her. Many of the older girls made her feel by every glance and word they gave her that she was taboo. And it was whispered on the campus that Amy would be sent home by Mrs. Tellingham, if she could not be made to pay, or her folks be made to pay, something toward the damage her carelessness had brought about.

Ruth sheltered the unfortunate Amy all she could. She even influenced her closest friends to be kind to the child. At Mrs. Sadoc Smith's Helen and Ann did not speak of the discovery of the origin of the fire, and, of course, good-natured Jennie Stone did just as Ruth asked, while even Mercy Curtis kept her lips closed.

Amy, however, not being an utterly callous girl, felt the condemnation of the whole school. There was no escaping that.

Amy had denied having a candle on the night of the fire, and it shocked and grieved Mrs. Tellingham very much to learn that one of her girls was not to be trusted to speak the truth at all times.

Not because of the fire did the preceptress consider sending Amy Gregg home, for the origin of the fire was plainly an accident, though bred in carelessness. For prevarication, however, Mrs. Tellingham was tempted to expel Amy Gregg.

The girl had denied the fact that she had left a candle burning in her room when she went to supper. Mary Pease had seen it, and both Miss Scrimp and Ruth Fielding knew that the fire started in that particular room.

Alice B. Emerson

Why the girl had left the candle burning was another mystery. Recklessly denying the main fact, of course Amy would not explain the secondary mystery. Nagged and heckled by some of the sophomores and juniors, Amy declared she wished the whole school had burned down and then she would not have had to stay at Briarwood another day!

Ruth and Helen one day rescued the girl from the midst of a mob of larger girls who were driving Amy Gregg almost mad by taunting her with being a "fire bug."

"What are you wild animals doing?" demanded Helen, who was much sharper with the evil doers among the under classes than was Ruth. "So she's a 'fire-bug?' Oh, girls! what better are you than poor little Gregg, I'd like to know? Every soul of you has done worse things than she has done—only your acts did not have such appalling results. Behave yourselves!"

Ruth could not have talked that way to the girls; but many of them slunk away under Helen's reprimand. Ruth took the crying Amy away—but neither she nor Helen was thanked.

"I wish you girls would mind your own business and let me alone," sobbed the foolish child, hysterically. "I can fight my own battles, I'll tear their hair out! I'll scratch their faces for them!"

"Oh, dear me, Amy!" sighed Ruth. "Do you think that would be any real satisfaction to you? Would it change things for the better, or in the least?"

What made the girls so unfeeling toward Amy was the fact that from the beginning she had expressed no sorrow over the destruction of the dormitory, and that she had refused to write home to ask for a contribution to the fund being raised for the new building.

When every other girl at Briarwood Hall was doing her best to get money to help Mrs. Tellingham, Amy Gregg's callousness regarding the fire and its results showed up, said Jennie, "just like a stubbed toe on a bare-footed boy!"

Really, Ruth began to think she would have to act as guard for Amy Gregg to and from the school. The girl was not allowed to play with the other girls of her age. Wherever she went a small riot started.

It had become general knowledge that Amy Gregg's father was a wealthy man, and that the family lived very sumptuously. Amy had a stepmother and several half brothers and sisters; but she did not get along well with them and, therefore, her father had sent her to Briarwood Hall.

"I guess she was too mean at home for them to stand her," said Mary Pease, who was the most vindictive of Amy's class, "and they sent her here to trouble *us*. And see what she's done!"

There was no stopping the younger girls from nagging. The fact that so much was being done by others to help the dormitory fund kept the feud against Amy Gregg alive. Her one partisan at this time (for Ruth could not be called that, no matter how sorry she was for her) was Curly Smith.

Once or twice Amy slipped away before Ruth was ready to go back to Mrs. Smith's house for the evening, and started alone for the lodgings. The Cedar Walk was the nearest way, and there were many hiding places along the Cedar Walk.

Mary Pease and her chums lay in wait for the unfortunate

Alice B. Emerson

Amy on two occasions, and chased her all the way to Mrs. Sadoc Smith's. What they intended doing to the much disliked girl if they had caught her, nobody seemed to know. They just seemed determined to plague her.

Ruth did not want to report the culprits; but warning them did not seem to do any good. On a third occasion Amy started home ahead, and Ruth and Helen hurried after her to make sure that none of the other girls troubled the victim. Half way down the walk, Helen exclaimed:

"See there, Ruth! Amy isn't alone, after all."

"Who's with her?" asked Ruth. "I can't see—Why! it can't be Ann?"

"No. But she's tall like Ann."

"And that girl walks queerly. Did you ever see the like? Strides along just like a boy—Oh!"

Out of a cedar clump appeared a crowd of shrieking girls, who began to dance around Amy and her companion, shouting scornful phrases which were bound to make Amy Gregg angry. But Mary and her friends this time received a surprise. Amy ran. Not so the "girl" with her.

This strange individual ran among Amy's tormentors, tripped two or three of them up, tore down the hair of several, taking the ribbons as trophies, and sent the whole crowd shrieking away, much alarmed and not a little punished.

"It isn't a girl!" gasped Helen. "It's Curly Smith. And as sure as you live he's got on some of Ann's clothes. *Won't* our Western friend be furious at that?"

But Ann Hicks was not troubled at all. She had lent Curly the frock and hat, and when he behaved himself and walked properly he certainly made a very pretty girl.

He gave Amy's enemies a good fright, and they let her alone after that.

"But, goodness me! what is Briarwood Hall coming to?" demanded Ruth, in discussing this incident with her room-mates. "We are leaving a tribe of young Indians here for Mrs. Tellingham to control. Helen! you know we never acted this way when we were in the lower grades."

"Well, we were pretty bad sometimes," Helen said slowly. "We did not engage in free fights, however."

"They all ought to have a good spanking," declared Ann, with conviction.

"And I suppose you seniors ought to do it?" sneered Amy, who could not be gentle even with her own friends.

"I'm not convinced that I sha'n't begin with you, my lady," said the Western girl, sharply. "I lent those old duds of mine to Curly to help you out, and you are about as grateful as a poison snake! I never saw such a girl in my life before."

CHAPTER XVIII

THE FIVE-REEL DRAMA

There was a spark of romance in old Mrs. Sadoc Smith, after all. Ruth read to her the first part of "The Heart of a School-girl" and to further the continuation and ultimate successful completion of that scenario, the old lady would have done much.

Curly looked upon Ruth with awe. He was a devotee of the moving pictures, and every nickel he could spare went into the coffers of one or the other of the "picture palaces" in Lumberton. Lumberton was a thriving city, with both water-freight and railroad facilities besides its mills and lumber interests; so it could well support several of the modern houses of entertainment that have sprung up in such mushroom growth all over the land.

Mr. Hammond's films taken at Lumberton were of an educational nature and the Board of Trade of the city expected much advertising of the industries of the place when the films were released.

However, to get back to Mrs. Sadoc Smith—Her instructions from Mrs. Tellingham included the putting out of the lamp in the big room the four Briarwood girls occupied by ten o'clock every night; but Mrs. Smith allowed Ruth to come downstairs after the other girls were in bed and write under the radiance of the reading lamp on her sitting-room table. It was quiet there, for Mrs. Sadoc Smith either sent Curly to bed, or made him keep as still as a mouse. And there was nobody else to disturb the young author as she wrote, save the cat that delighted to jump up into her lap and lie there purring, while the scenario was being written.

Ruth did not avail herself of this privilege often; but she was desirous for the scenario to be finished and in Mr. Hammond's hands. So sure had that gentleman been of her success, and so pleased was he with the plan of the entire play, that he had taken a copy of the first part with him when he left Lumberton and now wrote that Mr. Grimes was already making a few of the studio scenes.

The young author rather shrank from letting the pugnacious Mr. Grimes have anything to do with her story; but she knew that both Mr. Hammond and Hazel Gray thought highly of the man's ability. Nor was she in a position to insist upon any other director. She was working for Briarwood, not for her own advantage.

"If Grimes takes hold of it with his usual vigor, it will be a success," Mr. Hammond assured Ruth in his letter. "Hurry along the rest of the play. Spring is upon us, and we shall have some good open weather soon in which to take the pictures at Briarwood Hall."

Ruth hurried. Indeed, the story was finished so rapidly that the girl scarcely realized what she had done. There was no time for her to go over the scenario carefully for revision and polishing. The last scenes she read to nobody; she scarcely knew herself how they sounded.

Ruth Fielding had written an ingenious and very original scenario. Its crudities were many and manifest; nevertheless, the true gold was there. Mr. Hammond had recognized the originality of the girl's ideas in the first part of the play. He was not going into the scheme, and risking his money and reputation as a film producer, from any feeling of sentiment. It was a business proposition, pure and simple, with him.

In the first place, nobody had ever thought of just this kind of moving picture. The producer would be in the field with a new idea. In addition, the drama would be looked for all over the country by the friends of the pupils, past and present, of Briarwood Hall. The girls themselves appearing in some of the scenes would add to the interest their parents, friends, and the graduates of the Hall, were bound to take in the production.

To Ruth, nervous and overworked after the finishing of the scenario, the days of waiting until Mr. Hammond read and pronounced judgment on the play, were hard indeed to endure. No matter how much confidence her friends—even Mrs. Tellingham—had in her ability to succeed, Ruth was not at all sure she had written up to the mark.

Try as she might she began to fall behind in her recitation marks during these days of waiting. Her nervousness was enhanced by the doubts she felt regarding her general standing in her classes.

Mrs. Tellingham talked cheerfully in chapel about "our graduating class;" but some of the girls who were working with a view to receiving their diplomas in June would never be able to reach the high mark necessary for Mrs. Tellingham to allow them those certificates.

There would be a fringe of girls standing at the back of the class who, although never appearing at Briarwood Hall another term, could not win the roll of parchment which would enter them in good standing in any of the women's colleges. Ruth did not want to be among those who failed.

She worried about this a good deal; she could not sleep at night; and her cheeks grew pale. She worked hard, and yet sometimes when she reached the classroom she felt as though her head were a hollow drum in which the thoughts beat to and fro without either rhyme or reason.

Ruth Fielding was a perfectly healthy girl, as well as an athletic one. But in a time of stress like this the very healthiest person can easily and quickly break down. "I feel as though I should fly!" is an expression often heard from nervous and overwrought schoolgirls. Ruth wished that she might fly—away from school and study and scenarios and sullen girls like Amy Gregg.

One evening when she came back to Mrs. Sadoc Smith's with a strapful of books to study before bedtime, Ruth saw Curly Smith by the shed door busy with some fishing tackle. Ruth's pulses leaped. Fishing! She had not thrown a hook into the water for months and months!

"Going fishing, Curly?" she said wistfully.

"Yep."

"Where are they biting now?"

"There's carp and bream under the old mill-dam up in Norman's Woods. I saw 'em jumping there to-day."

"Oh! when are you going?" gasped the girl, hungry for outdoor sport and adventure.

"In the morning—before *you're* up," said the boy, rather sullenly.

"I wager I'll be awake," said Ruth, sitting down beside him. "I wake up—oh, just awfully early! and lie and think."

Curly looked at her. "That don't get you nothin'," he said.

"But I can't help it."

"Gran says you're overworked," Curly said. "Why don't you run away from school if they make you work so hard? *I* would. Our teacher's sick so there isn't any session at the district school to-morrow."

"Oh, Curly! Play hooky?" gasped Ruth, clasping her hands.

"Yep. Only you girls haven't any pluck."

"If I played hooky would you let me go fishing with you to-morrow?" asked Ruth, her eyes dancing.

"You haven't the sand," scoffed Curly.

"But can I go if I *dare* run away?" urged Ruth.

"Yep," said the boy, but with rather a sour grin.

"What time are you going to start?"

"Four."

"If I'm not down in the kitchen by that time, throw some gravel up to the window," commanded Ruth. "But don't break the window."

"Oh, shucks! you won't go when you see how dark and damp it is," declared Curly.

When, just after four o'clock in the morning, Curly crept downstairs from his shed chamber, knuckling his eyes to get the sleep out, there was a light in the kitchen and Ruth was just pouring out two fragrant cups of coffee which flanked a heaping plate of doughnuts.

"Old Scratch!" gasped Curly. "Gran will have our hides and hair! You're not *going*, Ruth Fielding?"

"If you will let me," said Ruth, meekly.

"Well—if you want. But you'll get wet and dirty and mussy—"

Then he stopped. He saw that Ruth had on an old gymnasium suit, her rubber boots lay on the chair, and a warm polo coat was at hand. She already wore her tam-o-shanter.

"Huh! I see you're ready," Curly said. "You might as well go. But remember, if you want to come home before afternoon, you'll have to find your way back alone. I'm not going to be bothered by a girl's fantods."

"All right, Curly," said Ruth, cheerfully.

Curly put his face under the spigot, brushed his hair before the little mirror in the corner, and was ready to sample Ruth's coffee.

"We want to hurry," he said, filling his pockets with the doughnuts, "it'll be broad daylight before we know it, and then everybody we see will want to come along. The other fellows aren't on to the old dam yet this season. The fish are running early."

He brought forth a basket with tackle and bait, dug over night. Ruth burdened herself with a big, square box, neatly wrapped and tied. Curly eyed this askance.

"I s'pose you expect to tear your clo'es and want something to wear back to town that's decent," he growled.

"Well, I want to look half way respectable," laughed Ruth, as they set forth.

The damp smell of thawing earth greeted their nostrils as they left the house. No plowing had been done, save in very warm corners; but the lush buds on the trees and bushes, and the crocuses by the corner of the old house, promised spring.

A clape called at them raucously as he rapped out his warning on a dead limb beside the road. A rabbit rose from its form and shot away into the dripping woods. The sun poked a jolly red face above the wooded ridge before the two runaways left the beaten track and took a narrow woodpath that would cut off about a mile of their walk.

It was a rough way and the pace Curly set was made to force Ruth to beg for time. But the girl gritted her teeth, minded not the pain in her side, and sturdily followed him. By and by the pain stopped, she got her second wind, and then she began to tread close on Curly's heels.

"Huh!" he grunted at last, "you needn't be in such a hurry. The dam will stay there—and so will the fish."

"All right," responded Ruth, still meekly, but with dancing eyes.

The fishing place was reached and while yet the early rays of the sun fell aslant the dimpling pools under the dam, the two threw in their baited hooks. Curly evidently expected to see the girl balk at the bait, but Ruth seized firmly the fat, squirmy worm and impaled it scientifically upon her hook.

She caught the first fish, too! In fact, as the morning drew leisurely along, Ruth's string splashing in the cool water grew much faster than Curly's.

"I never saw the beat of your luck!" declared the boy. "You must have been fishing before, Ruth Fielding."

"Lots of times."

"Where?"

Ruth told him of the Red Mill on the bank of the Lumano, of her fishing trips with Tom Cameron, and of all the fun that they had about Cheslow, and up the river above the mill.

Mid-forenoon came and Curly produced some crackers and a piece of bologna. The doughnuts he had pocketed were gone long ago.

"Have a bite, Ruth?" he said generously. "I wish it was better, but I didn't have much money, and Gran won't ever let me carry any lunch. She says the proper place for a boy to eat is at his own table. It's there for me, and if I don't get home to get it, then I can do without."

Ruth accepted a piece of the bologna and the crackers gravely. She baited her hook with a piece of the bologna and caught a big, struggling carp.

"What do you know about that?" cried Curly, in disgust.

Alice B. Emerson

"You could bait your hook with a marble and catch a whopper, I believe!"

Meanwhile, Ruth was having a most delightful time. The roses had come back into her cheeks at the first. Her eyes sparkled, and she "wriggled all over," as she expressed it, "with just the *feel* of spring."

She did not spend all her time fishing, but ran about and examined the early plants and sprouting bushes, and woke up the first violets and searched for May flowers, which, of course, she did not find. Squirrels chattered at them, and a blue jay hung about, squalling, evidently hoping for crumbs from their lunch. Only there were no crumbs of Curly's frugal bologna and crackers left.

When the sun was in mid-heaven the boy confessed to being as hungry as ever, and tightened his belt. "Crackers don't stick to your ribs much," he grumbled.

Ruth calmly began opening her box. Curly looked at her askance.

"You aren't figgering on going home *now*, are you?" he asked.

"Oh, no. I sha'n't go home till you do."

Then she produced from the box sandwiches, deviled eggs, a jelly roll, a jar of peanut butter, crackers, olives, and some more of Mrs. Smith's good doughnuts.

"Old Scratch!" Curly ejaculated. "You're the best fellow to go fishing with, Ruth Fielding, that I ever saw. You can come to *my* parties any time you like."

They spent the whole day delightfully and, tired, scratched, and not a little wind-burned, Ruth tramped home behind Curly in good season for supper at Mrs. Sadoc Smith's.

She did not tell the boy that the whole outing had been arranged the night before with his grandmother before Ruth herself went to bed. Curly expected to be "called down," as he expressed it, by his grandmother when they arrived home. To his amazement they were met cheerfully and ushered in to a bounteous supper on which Mrs. Smith had expended no little thought and time.

Curly was stricken almost dumb by his grandmother's generosity and good-nature. After supper he whispered to Ruth:

"Say! you're a wonder, you are, Ruth Fielding. Never anybody got around Gran the way you do, before. You're a wonder!"

Helen and Ann met Ruth in great excitement. "Where under the sun have you been—and in that ragged old gym suit?" gasped Helen.

"You look as though your face was burnt. I believe you've been playing hooky, Ruth Fielding!" cried Ann.

"Right the first time," sighed Ruth, happily. "Oh, I feel *so* much better. And I know I shall sleep like a brick."

"You mean, a railroad tie, don't you?" demanded Ann. "*That's* a sleeper!"

"Of course we found your note, and we told Miss Brokaw. But she's got it in for you just the same," said Helen, slangily. "And only guess!"

Alice B. Emerson

"Yes! Guess! Ruth! Fielding!" and Ann seized her and danced her about the room. "You missed it by being absent to-day."

"Oh, don't! Never mind all this! I'm tired enough. I've walked *miles*," groaned Ruth. "What have I missed?"

"Mr. Hammond is in Lumberton. He came to see you about the scenario," Helen eagerly said.

Ruth sat down and clasped her hands, while her cheeks paled. "It's a failure!" she whispered.

CHAPTER XIX

GREAT TIMES

That was not so, however, and Helen and Ann soon blurted out the good news:

"It's a great success!"

"He's going to bring up the company next week and make the pictures at the Hall!"

"He's been with Mrs. Tellingham all the afternoon planning when the pictures shall be taken, and how they shall be taken," Helen said. "I guess it's *not* a failure!"

"I should say not!" joined in Ann Hicks.

"Oh, girls!"

If it had not been for Ruth's long day in the open and the fact that her nerves had become much quieter, she could never have forced back the tears of relief that answered so quickly these reassuring words.

Then a great flood of thankfulness welled up in her heart. She had accomplished something really worth while! Later, when she saw, on the screen, the story she had written, she was to feel this gratitude and joy again.

She went to bed that night and slept, as she had promised, until Mrs. Sadoc Smith knocked on the door for them all to rise. She got up with all the oppression lifted from her mind, and wanted to race the other girls to the Hall before breakfast.

"It won't do for you, young lady, to go gallavanting into the woods with Curly another day," said Helen, holding on to Ruth. "You're neither to hold nor to bind after such an expedition. I say, girls, let's all go with Curly next time."

Amy had been very sullen ever since the evening before. Now she snapped: "I guess Curly didn't want her—or any of us. Ruth just forced herself upon him. He doesn't like girls."

"Bless the infant!" said Ann. "What's got her *now*?"

"Jealous of our Ruth, I declare!" laughed Helen.

Amy burst out crying and ran ahead, nor did the older girls see her at the breakfast table. Ruth was sorry about this. She had only then begun to win Amy Gregg's confidence, and now she feared that the girl would be angry with her.

That day, however, Ruth was too happy to think much about Amy Gregg.

Recitations went with a rush. Miss Brokaw even was disarmed, for all Ruth's quickness and coolness seemed to have returned to her. She did not fail once and the strict teacher praised her.

Besides, there was a long conference with Mrs. Tellingham

and Mr. Hammond. The scenario of "The Heart of a Schoolgirl" was to be filmed at once.

"We will do our best to release it for first presentation in six weeks," the producer said. "And I assure you that means some quick work. You girls," he added, to Ruth, "must do your prettiest when we take the pictures here. Your physical culture instructor will drill you in marching, and forming the tableaux we require. Your exposition of the legend of the Marble Harp is a clever bit of invention, Ruth, and in the picture will make a hit, I am sure."

Of course Ruth was proud; why should she not be? But her head was not turned by all the flattering things that were said to her.

The girls adored her. The fact that they were all working in unison toward the rebuilding of the dormitory, removed from the daily life and intercourse of the big boarding school one of its more unpleasant features.

It was only natural that there should be cliques among two hundred girls. But now rivalries were put aside. All were striving for the same end. Some of the girls interested various societies in their home towns to hold fairs and bazaars for the benefit of Briarwood Hall.

Personal appeals were made directly to every girl on the alumni list—and some of those "girls" now had girls of their own almost old enough to attend Briarwood.

By these methods the dormitory fund was swelled. In the results from the moving picture drama, however, was the possibility for the greatest help. Mrs. Tellingham risked rebuilding the dormitory on the same scale as the burned structure, because of Mr. Hammond's enthusiasm over

Alice B. Emerson

Ruth's achievement.

The days of early spring passed in swift procession now. It seemed that the longer the days grew, the faster they seemed to go. There were not hours enough in which to accomplish all that the girls, who looked toward graduation in June, wished.

Even Jennie Stone worked harder and took her school tasks more seriously than ever before.

"But, see here!" she said to her mates one day, "here's some 'hot ones' Miss Brokaw has been handing the primes, and I believe they'd puzzle some of us big girls. Listen! 'What is longitude?' Sue Mellen came to me, puzzled, about *that*," chuckled Jennie, "and I told her longitude is those lengthwise stripes on a watermelon."

"Oh, Heavy!" gasped Lluella. "How could you?"

"Didn't hurt me at all," proclaimed Jennie, calmly. "And I told her that a 'ski' is what a Russian has on the end of his name. That quite satisfiedski Miss Mellenski, whether it does Miss Brokawski or not!"

Mrs. Tellingham gave the school a serious talk the day before the film company arrived to take the first pictures for Ruth's play. She read and explained that part of the scenario in which the Briarwood girls would appear, and begged their serious co-operation with the director who would have the making of the film in charge.

Ruth still shrank from seeing Mr. Grimes again; but she found that, while engaged in the work of making these pictures, he behaved quite differently from the way he had acted the day she had first seen him on the bank of the

Lumano river.

He was patient, but insistent. He knew just what effect he wanted and always got it in the end. And Ruth and Helen told each other that, ugly as he could be, Mr. Grimes was really a most wonderful director. They did not wonder that Hazel Gray expressed her desire to work under Mr. Grimes, harsh as he had been to her.

It was difficult for the girls—even for Ruth who had written the scenario—to follow the trend of the story of "The Heart of a Schoolgirl" by closely watching the taking of these scenes in and about Briarwood Hall; for they were not taken in proper rotation.

Mr. Grimes had his schedule before him and he skipped from one part of the story's action to another in a most bewildering way, getting the scenes about the school filmed in each "setting" in succession, rather than following the thread of the story.

Nor could Ruth judge the effect of the several pictures. She was too close to them. There was no perspective.

Sometimes when Mr. Grimes seemed the most satisfied, Ruth could see nothing in that scene at all. Again he would make the participants go over and over a scene that seemed perfectly clear the first time.

Hazel Gray and several other professional performers were at Briarwood and had their parts in the scenes with the schoolgirls. Hazel played the heroine of Ruth's drama, but Mr. Hammond had insisted upon Ruth herself acting the part of the heroine's chum—a not unimportant role.

Ruth did not feel that she had histrionic ability; but she was so anxious for the moving picture to be a success, that she would have tried her very best to suit Mr. Grimes in any role. She was surprised, however, when he warmly praised her work in her one scene which was at all emotional.

"You naturally feel your part in this scene, Miss Fielding," he said. "Not everybody could get the action before the camera so well."

"'Praise from Sir Hubert!'" whispered Hazel Gray, smiling at her young friend. "You should be proud."

Ruth was not quite sure whether she was proud of this unsuspected talent or not. She had written to Aunt Alvirah about her acting in the play, and the good woman had warned her seriously against the folly of vanity and the sin of frivolity. Aunt Alvirah had been brought up to doubt very much the morality of those who performed upon the stage for the amusement of the public.

What Mr. Jabez Potter thought of his niece's acting for the screen, even his opinion of her writing a play, was a sealed matter to Ruth; for the old miller, as Aunt Alvirah informed her, grew grumpier and more morose all the time. "He is a caution to get along with," wrote Aunt Alvirah Boggs in her cramped handwriting. "I don't know what's going to become of him. You'd think he was weaned on wormwood and drunk nothing but boneset tea all his life long."

However, it must be confessed that Ruth Fielding's thoughts were not much upon her Uncle Jabez or the Red Mill these days. The work of making the pictures occupied all her thought that was not taken up with study.

Jennie Stone, Sarah Fish, Helen, Lluella and Belle, all appeared prominently in the "close up" scenes Mr. Grimes took. In the classroom, dining hall, the graduation march, and in the Italian garden scenes, most of the seniors and juniors were used.

A splendid gymnasium scene pleased the girls, and views of the hand-ball, captain's-ball, tennis and basket-ball courts, with the girls in action, were bound to be spectacular, too.

These typical boarding school scenes closely followed the text of Ruth's play. Hazel and Ruth were in them all; and on the tennis court Hazel and Ruth played Helen and Sarah Fish a fast game, the former couple winning by sheer skill and pluck.

Ruth naturally had to neglect some duties. Discipline was more or less relaxed, and she lost sight of Amy Gregg.

One evening the smaller girl did not appear at Mrs. Sadoc Smith's after supper. Of late the other girls had let Amy Gregg alone and Ruth had ceased to watch her so carefully. But when darkness fell and Amy did not appear, Ruth telephoned to the school. Miss Scrimp, who answered the call, had not seen her. It was learned, too, that Amy had not been at the supper table. Nobody had seen her depart, but it was a fact that she had disappeared from Briarwood Hall sometime during the afternoon. Nor had she been near Mrs. Sadoc Smith's since early morning.

CHAPTER XX

A CLOUD ARISES

While Mrs. Smith and Helen and Ann Hicks were "running around in circles," as Ann put it, wondering what had become of Amy Gregg, Ruth did the only practical thing she could think of.

She hunted up Curly.

"Old Scratch!" ejaculated the boy. "I haven't seen Amy to-day. Sure I haven't! No, Ma'am!"

"Not at *all*?" asked Ruth. "And don't you know where to look for her?"

"Oh, she'll take care of herself," said the boy, carelessly. "She isn't as soft as most girls."

"But Mrs. Tellingham will be awfully angry with me," Ruth cried. "I was supposed to look out for her when she came over here."

"Shucks!" exclaimed Curly. "Amy didn't want to be looked out for."

"That doesn't absolve me from my duty," sighed Ruth. "Haven't you the least idea where she's gone?"

"No, Ruth, I haven't," the boy declared earnestly. "If I had I'd tell you."

"I believe you, Curly."

"She and I haven't been so friendly," admitted the boy, in some embarrassment, "since you went fishing with me that time."

"Goodness me! she's not jealous?" cried Ruth.

"I don't know what you call it," said Curly, hanging his head. "It's some foolish girl stuff. Boys don't act that way. I told her I'd take her fishing, too—if she'd get up early enough." Here Curly began to laugh. "You can bet, Ruth, that wherever she is, she got there before dark and won't come back until daylight."

"What do you mean?" asked Ruth, sharply.

"I know she's afraid as she can be of the dark. She's a regular baby about that. Of course, she won't own up to it."

"Why! I never knew it," Ruth exclaimed.

"She wouldn't go fishing because I start so early—while it's still dark. Catch *her* out of the house before sun-up!"

"Oh, Curly! I blame myself," gasped Ruth. "I never knew that about her. Are you sure?"

"'Course I am. She's scared of the dark. I can make her mad any time by just hinting at it. So that proves it, don't it?"

responded this young philosopher.

"Maybe she has gone somewhere and is afraid to come back till morning," repeated Ruth.

"She's been after me to take her up to that dam where we caught the fish, in the afternoon; but I told her we couldn't get home before pitch dark. I ought to have taken her along, I guess, and said nothing," Curly added reflectively.

"Last night she was talking about it. She said I should take her because I took you there."

"You don't suppose she's gone clear over there by herself, do you?" Ruth cried, in alarm.

"I don't believe she knows how to start, even," Curly said easily. "And I told her last night she'd better not go anywhere till she got rid of that sore throat."

"Sore throat!" repeated Ruth, with added worriment. "I never knew her throat was sore."

"She told me, she did," Curly said. "It was pretty bad, I guess, too. I guess maybe she was afraid to say anything about it. I don't like to tell Gran when there's anything the matter with me. She mixes up such nasty messes for me to take!"

"The poor child!" murmured Ruth, thinking only of Amy Gregg. "What *shall* we do?"

"I'll get a lantern and we'll go hunt around for her," suggested Curly, ripe for any adventure.

"But where will we hunt?"

"Maybe she's gone with some other girl somewhere."

"You know that can't be so," Ruth said. "There isn't a girl friendly enough with her for her to say ten pleasant words to. The poor little mite! I'm just as sorry as I can be for her, Curly."

"Well!" returned Curly, "what did she want to tell a story for? I know what she did. She left the candle burning in her room because she was afraid to come back to it in the dark after supper. I made her own up to that."

"Oh! the poor child!" cried Ruth.

"And she didn't understand the electric light. They don't have electricity in the town where she comes from; natural gas, instead. So that's the *why* of the fire," Curly said. "I picked that out of her long ago."

"And she was so close-mouthed with us!" exclaimed Ruth.

"She doesn't like it at Briarwood. She doesn't like the girls. She doesn't like the teachers. Old Scratch!" exclaimed the boy, "I don't blame her—and I guess I'd run away myself."

"You don't suppose she *has* run away, Curly Smith? Not for *keeps*?"

"I don't know," answered the boy. "Her folks don't treat her right, I guess. They sent her to Briarwood to get her out the way. So she says. And she's afraid of what her father will do to her if he ever hears about that candle and about how the dormitory got afire."

"That's why she wouldn't write to him for a contribution to the rebuilding fund," cried Ruth.

Alice B. Emerson

"I guess so," said Curly. "She never said much to me about it. I just wormed it out of her, as you might say. She isn't so awful happy here, you bet."

"Oh, Curly! I blame myself," groaned Ruth.

"What for?"

"Because I ought to have learned more about her—got closer to her."

"You might's well try to get close to a prickly porcupine," laughed the boy. "She'd made up her mind to hate the rest of you girls and she's going to keep on hating you till the end of time. That's the sort of a girl Amy is."

"And nothing to be proud about," declared Ruth, with some vexation. "Don't you think it, Curly?"

"Huh! I don't. You're silly, Ruth—but I like you a whole lot more than I do Amy."

"Goodness! what a polite boy," cried Ruth. "There's the telephone!"

She ran back upstairs, hoping the message would be that Amy Gregg was found. But that was not it. Over the wire Mrs. Tellingham herself was speaking to Ann.

"No, Ma'am. We don't know where to look for her," Ann said.

"We haven't any idea."

"Yes, Ma'am; Helen and I have looked. She hasn't taken any of her clothes."

"Oh, goodness! you don't really suppose she's run away?"

"Do come here, Ruth, and hear what Mrs. Tellingham says!"

Ruth went to the telephone and heard the principal of Briarwood Hall talking. What Mrs. Tellingham said was certainly startling.

It seemed that Amy Gregg had received a letter that afternoon. It was from her father, and, of course, was not opened by the principal. But afterward—after the child had disappeared from the premises, of course—the letter came into Mrs. Tellingham's hands. It was found by Tony Foyle down by the marble statue in the sunken garden. Evidently Amy had run there, where she would be out of the way, to read it.

It was a very stern letter and accused Amy of some past offense before she had left home. It likewise said that Mr. Gregg had received an anonymous letter from some girl at Briarwood, telling about the fire, and about Amy's supposed part in starting the blaze, and complaining that Amy would not ask for a contribution to the dormitory fund.

Mr. Gregg was extremely angry, and he told his daughter that he would come to Briarwood in a few days and investigate the whole matter. Why Amy Gregg should run away was now clear. She was afraid to meet her father.

"Make sure that the poor child is nowhere about Mrs. Smith's, Ruth," Mrs. Tellingham begged her over the wire. "I am sure I should not know what to say to Mr. Gregg if he comes and finds that his daughter has disappeared. The poor child! I shall not sleep to-night, Ruth Fielding. Amy must be found."

Alice B. Emerson

Ruth felt just that way herself. No matter what her friends said in contradiction, Ruth felt that she was partly to blame. She should have kept a close watch over Amy Gregg.

"I let that picture-making get in between us," she wailed. "I'm glad it's all done and out of the way. I'd rather not have written the scenario at all, than have anything happen to Amy."

"You're a goose, Ruthie," declared her chum. "You're not to blame. Her father's harshness with her has made the child run away. *If* she has."

"Her own unhappy disposition has caused all the trouble," said Ann, bitterly.

"Oh! don't speak so," begged Ruth. "Suppose something has happened to her."

"Nothing ever happens to kids like her," said Ann, bruskly.

But that was not so. Something already had happened to Amy Gregg. She was lost!

CHAPTER XXI

HUNTING FOR AMY

In spite of her seemingly heartless words, it was Ann Hicks who agreed to go with Ruth to hunt for the lost girl. Helen frankly acknowledged that she was afraid to tramp about the woods and fields at night, with only a boy and a lantern for company.

"Come along, Ruthie. I have helped find stray cattle on the range more times than you could shake a stick at," declared good-natured Ann Hicks. "Rouse out that lazy boy of Grandma Smith's."

Mrs. Sadoc Smith had to give just so much advice, and see that the expedition was properly equipped. A thermos bottle filled with coffee went into Ruth's bag, while Curly was laden with a substantial lunch, a roll of bandages, a bottle of arnica and some smelling-salts, beside the lantern.

"Huh!" protested the boy to Ann, "if she was sending us out to find a lost *boy* all she'd send would be that cat-o'-nine-tails of hers that hangs in the woodshed. I know Gran!"

"And the cat-o'-nine-tails, too, eh?" chuckled the Western girl.

"You bet!" agreed Curly, feelingly.

They set forth with just one idea about the search. Amy Gregg, as far as Curly could remember, had expressed a wish to go to but one place. That was the old dam up in Norman's Woods, where he and Ruth had gone fishing.

They were quite sure that it would be useless to hunt for the girl in any neighbor's house. And Mrs. Sadoc Smith's premises had already been searched. They had shouted for Amy till their throats were sore before the news had come from Briarwood Hall. The fact that Amy had been suffering from a physical ailment, as well as one of the mind, troubled Ruth exceedingly.

"Maybe she was just 'sickening for some disease,' as Aunt Alvirah says," the girl of the Red Mill told Ann Hicks, as they went along. "A sore throat is the forerunner of so many fevers and serious troubles. She might be coming down with scarlet fever."

"Goodness gracious! don't say *that*" begged Ann.

Ruth feared it, nevertheless. The two girls followed Curly through the narrow path, the dripping bushes wetting their skirts, and briers at times scratching them. Ann was a good walker and could keep up quite as well as Ruth. Beside, Curly was not setting a pace on this occasion, but stumbled on with the lantern, rather blindly.

"Tell you what," he grumbled. "I don't fancy this job a mite."

"You're not 'afraid to go home in the dark,' are you, Curly?" asked Ann, with scorn.

"Not going home just now," responded the boy, grinning.

"But the woods aren't any place to be out in this time of night—unless you've got a dog and a gun. There! see that?"

"A cat, that's all," declared Ruth, who had seen the little black and white animal run across their track in the flickering and uncertain light of the lantern. "Here, kitty! kitty! Puss! puss! puss!"

"Hold on!" cried the excited Curly. "You needn't be so particular about calling that cat."

"Why not? It must be somebody's cat that's strayed," said Ruth.

"Ya-as. I guess it is. It's a pole-cat," growled Curly. "And if it came when you called it, you wouldn't like it so much, I guess."

"Oh, goodness!" gasped Ann. "Don't be so friendly with every strange animal you see, Ruth Fielding. A pole-cat!"

"Wish I had a gun!" exclaimed Curly. "I'd shoot that skunk."

"Glad you didn't then," said Ruth, promptly. "Poor little thing."

"Ya-as," drawled the boy. "'Poor little thing.' It was just aiming for somebody's hencoop. One of 'em 'll eat chickens faster than Gran's hens can hatch 'em out."

Pushing on through the woods at this slow pace brought them to the ruined grist mill and the old dam not before ten o'clock. There was a pale and watery moon, the shine of which glistened on the falling water over the old logs of the dam, but gave the searchers little light. The moon's rays merely aided in making the surroundings of the mill

Alice B. Emerson

more ghostly.

Nobody lived within a mile of the mill site, Curly assured the girls, and if Amy had found this place it was not likely that she had likewise found the nearest human habitation, for that was beyond the mill and directly opposite to Briarwood and the town of Lumberton.

They shouted for Amy, and then searched the ghostly premises of the ruined mill. Years before the roof had been burned away and some of the walls fallen in. Owls made their nests in the upper part of the building, as the party found, much to the girls' excitement when a huge, spread-winged creature dived out of a window and went "whish! whish! whish!" off through the long grass, to hunt for mice or other small, night-prowling creatures.

"Goodness! that owl is as big as a turkey!" gasped Ruth, clinging to Ann in her fright.

"Bigger," announced Curly. "Old Scratch! I'd like to shoot him and have him stuffed."

"I'd rather have some of the turkey stuffing," chuckled Ann Hicks. "Owl would be rather tough, I reckon."

"Oh, not to eat!" scoffed Curly. "I'd put him in Gran's parlor. And that reminds me of an owl story—"

"Don't tell us any old stories; tell us new ones, if you must tell any," Ann interrupted.

"How do you know whether this is old or young till I've told it?" demanded Curly, as they all three sat on the ruined doorstep of the mill to rest.

"Quite right, Curly," sighed Ruth. "Go ahead. Make us laugh. I feel like crying."

"Then you can cry over it," retorted the boy. "There was a butcher who had a stuffed owl in his shop and an old Irishman came in and asked him: 'How mooch for the broad-faced bur-r-rd?'

"'It's an owl,' said the butcher.

"The old man repeated his question—'how mooch for the broad-faced bur-r-rd?'

"'It's an owl, I tell you!' exclaimed the butcher.

"'I know it's *ould*,' says the Irishman. 'But what d'ye want for it? It'll make soup for me boar-r-rders!'"

"That's a good story," admitted Ruth, "but try to think up some way of finding poor little Amy, instead of telling funny tales."

"Oh, how can I help—"

Curly stopped. Ann, who was sitting in the middle, grabbed both him and Ruth. "Listen to that!" she whispered. "*that* isn't another owl, is it?"

"What is it?" gasped Ruth.

Somewhere in the ruin of the mill there was a noise. It might have been the voice of an animal or of a bird, but it sounded near enough like a human being to scare all three of the young people on the doorstep.

"Sa-ay," quavered Curly. "You don't suppose there are such

things as ghosts, do you, girls?"

"No, I don't!" snapped Ruth. "Don't try to scare us either, Curly."

"Honest, I'm not. I'm right here," cried the boy. "You know I never made that noise—"

"There it is again!" exclaimed Ann.

The sound was like the cry of something in distress. Ruth got up suddenly and tried to put on a brave front. "I can't sit here and listen to that," she said.

"Let's go," urged Ann. "I'm ready."

"Oh, say—" began Curly, when Ruth interrupted him by seizing the lantern.

"Don't fret, Curly Smith," she said. "We're not going without finding out what that sound means."

"Maybe it's young owls, and the old one will come back and pick our eyes out," suggested Ann.

"Get a club, Curly," commanded Ruth. "We'll be ready, then, for man or beast."

This order gave Curly confidence, and made him pluck up his own waning courage. These girls depended upon him, and he was not the boy to back down before even a ghostly Unknown.

He found a club and went side by side with Ruth into the mill. The sound that had disturbed them was repeated. Ruth was sure, now, that it was somebody sobbing.

"Amy! Amy Gregg!" she called again.

"Pshaw!" murmured Ann. "It isn't Amy. She'd have been out of here in a hurry when we shouted for her before."

Ruth was not so sure of that. They came to a break in the flooring. Once there had been steps here leading down into the cellar of the mill, but the steps had rotted away.

"Amy!" called Ruth again. She knelt and held the lantern as far down the well as she could reach. The sound of sobbing had ceased.

"Amy, *dear*!" cried Ruth. "It's Ruth and Ann, And Curly is with us. Do answer if you hear me!"

There was a murmur from below. Ann cried out in alarm, but Curly exclaimed: "I believe that's Amy, Ruth! She must be hurt—the silly thing. She's tumbled down this old well."

"How will we get to her?" cried Ruth. "Amy! how did you get down there? Are you hurt, Amy?"

"Go away!" said a faint voice from below.

"Old Scratch! Isn't that just like her?" groaned Curly. "She was hiding from us."

"Here," said Ruth, drawing up the lantern and setting it on the floor. "It can't be very deep. I'm going to drop down there, Curly, and then you pass down the lantern to me."

"You'll break your neck, Ruth!" cried Ann.

"No. I'm not going to risk my neck at all," Ruth calmly affirmed.

Alice B. Emerson

She set the lantern on the broken floor and swung herself down into the black hole. She hung by her hands and her feet did not touch the bottom. Suddenly she felt a qualm of terror. Perhaps the cellar was a good deal deeper than she had supposed!

She could not raise herself up again, and she almost feared to drop. "Let down the light, Curly!" she whispered.

CHAPTER XXII

DISASTER THREATENS

Before Curly could comply with Ruth's whispered request, her fingers slipped on the edge of the flooring. "Oh!" she cried out, and—dropped as much as three inches!

"Goodness me, Ruth!" gasped Ann Hicks. "Are you killed?"

"No—o. But I might as well have been as to be scared to death," declared the girl of the Red Mill. "I never thought the cellar was so shallow."

There was a rustling near by. Ruth thought of rats and almost screamed aloud. "Give me the lantern—quick!" she called up to Curly Smith.

"Here you are," said that youth. "And if Amy is down there she ought to be ashamed of herself—making us so much trouble."

Amy was there, as Ruth saw almost immediately when she could throw the radiance of the lantern about her. But Ruth did not feel like scolding the younger girl.

Amy had crept away into a corner. Her movements made the

Alice B. Emerson

rustling Ruth had heard. She hid her face against her arm and sobbed with abandonment. Her dress was torn and muddy, her shoes showed that she had waded in mire. She had lost her hat and her flaxen hair was a tangle of briers and green burrs.

"My *dear*!" cried Ruth, kneeling down beside her. "What does it mean? Why did you come here? Oh, you're sick!"

A single glance at the flushed face and neck of the smaller girl, and a tentative touch upon her wrist, assured Ruth of that last fact. Amy seemed burning up with fever. Ruth had never seen a case of scarlet fever, but she feared that might be Amy's trouble.

"How long have you been here?" she asked Amy.

"Si—since—since it got dark," choked the girl.

"Is your throat sore?" asked Ruth, anxiously.

"Yes, it is; aw—awful sore."

"And you're feverish," said Ruth.

"I—I'm aw—all shivery, too," wept Amy Gregg, quite given up to misery now.

Ruth was confident that the smaller girl had developed the fever that she feared. Chill, fever, sore throat, and all, made the diagnosis seem quite reasonable.

"How did you get into this cellar?" she asked Amy.

"There's a hole in the underpinning over yonder," said the culprit.

"Come on, then; we'll get out that way. Can you walk?"

"Oh—oh—yes," choked Amy.

She proved this by immediately starting out of the cellar. Ruth lit the way with the lantern.

"Hi!" shouted Curly Smith, "where are you going with that light?"

"Come back to the door," commanded Ruth's muffled voice in the cellar. "You can find your way all right."

"What do you know about that?" demanded Ann. "Leaves us in the lurch for that miserable child, who ought to be walloped."

"Oh, Ann, don't say that!" cried Ruth, as she and the sick girl appeared at the mill door. "No! don't come near us. I'll carry the lantern myself and lead Amy. She's not feeling well, but she can walk. We must get her to Mrs. Smith's just as soon as possible and call a doctor."

"What's the matter with her?" demanded Curly, curiously.

"She feels bad. That's enough," said Ruth, shortly. "Come on, Amy."

For once Amy Gregg was glad to accept Ruth Fielding's help. She had no idea what Ruth thought was the matter with her, and she stumbled on beside the older girl, sleepy and ill, given up to utter misery. Curly and Ann began to be suspicious when Ruth forbade them to approach Amy and herself.

"Old Scratch!" whispered the boy to the Western girl. "I bet

Amy's got small-pox or something. Ruth Fielding will catch it, too."

"Hush!" exclaimed Ann, fiercely. "It's not as bad as that."

It was a long walk to Mrs. Sadoc Smith's. At the last, Ruth almost carried Amy, who was not a particularly small girl. Curly grabbed the lantern and insisted upon walking close to them.

"No matter if I *do* catch the epizootic; guess I'll get over it," said the boy.

They finally came to the Smith house. Helen and Mrs. Sadoc Smith came out on the porch when the dog barked. Ruth made Ann and Curly go ahead and held back with the sick girl.

"You go right upstairs with Helen, Ann," commanded Ruth. "I want to talk to Mrs. Smith about Amy. She must be put in a warm room downstairs."

Mrs. Sadoc Smith agreed to this proposal the instant she saw Amy's flushed face and heard her muttering.

"You telephone for Doctor Lambert, Henry," commanded Mrs. Smith. "We'll have him give a look at her—though I could dose her myself, I reckon, and bring her out all right."

Ruth feared the worst. She secretly stuck to her first diagnosis that Amy had scarlet fever, but she did not say this to Mrs. Smith. They put Amy to bed between blankets, and Mrs. Smith succeeded in getting the girl to drink a dose of hot tea.

"That'll start her perspiring, which won't do a bit of harm," she said to Ruth. "But I never saw anybody's face so red before—and her hands and arms, too. She's breaking all out, I do declare."

Ruth was thinking: "If they have to quarantine Amy, I'll be quarantined with her. I'll have to nurse her instead of going to school. Poor little thing! she will require somebody's constant attention.

"But, oh dear!" added the girl of the Red Mill, "what will become of my school work? I'll never be able to graduate in the world. Lucky those moving pictures are taken—I won't be needed any more in those. Oh, dear!"

Ruth did not allow a murmur to escape her lips, however. She insisted on remaining by the patient all night, too. Mrs. Smith was not able to quiet the sick girl as well as Ruth did when the delirium Amy developed became wilder.

It was almost daylight before Dr. Lambert came. He had been out of town on a case, but came at once when he returned to Lumberton and found the call from Mrs. Sadoc Smith's.

"What is it, Doctor?" asked the old lady. "She's as red as a lobster. Is it anything catching? This girl ought not to be here, if it is."

"This girl had better remain here till we find out just what is the matter," the doctor returned, scowling in a puzzled way at the patient. He had seen at once that Ruth could control Amy.

"But what is it?"

"Fever. Delirium. You can see for yourself. What its name is,

I'll tell you when I come again. Keep on just as you are doing, and give her this soothing medicine, and plenty of cracked ice—on her tongue, at least. That is what is the matter; she is consumed with thirst. I'll have to see that eruption again before I can say for sure what the matter is."

He went, and left the house in a turmoil of excitement. Helen and Ann did not wish to go to Briarwood and leave Ruth; but Mrs. Tellingham commanded them to. Much to his delight, Curly was kept out of his school to run errands.

Ruth got a nap on the lounge in the sitting room, and felt better. The doctor returned at nine o'clock in the forenoon and by that time the sick girl's face was so swollen that she could scarcely see out of her eyes. Her hands and wrists were puffed badly, too.

"Where has she been?" demanded Dr. Lambert.

Ruth told him what they supposed had happened to Amy the day before and where she had been found late at night.

"Humph!" grunted the medical practitioner. "That's what I thought. Effect of the *Rhus Toxicodendron*. Bad case."

This sounded very terrible to Ruth until she suddenly remembered something she had read in her botany. A great feeling of relief came over her.

"Oh! poison-ash!" she cried.

"Good land! Nothin' but poison ivy?" demanded Mrs. Sadoc Smith.

"Poison oak, or poison sumac—whatever you have a mind to call it. But a bad case of it, I assure you. I'll leave more of the cooling draught; and I'll send up a salve to put on her face and hands. Don't let it get into the poor child's eyes—and don't let her tear off the mask which she will have to wear."

"Then there is no danger of scarlet fever," whispered Ruth, feeling relieved.

Alice B. Emerson

CHAPTER XXIII

PUTTING ONE'S BEST FOOT FORWARD

Amy Gregg's escapade created a lot of excitement at Briarwood Hall. Inasmuch as it affected Ruth, the whole school was in a flutter about it.

Helen and Ann had come to the Hall, late for breakfast, and spread the news in the dining hall. They were both sure, by Ruth's actions and the doctor's first noncommittal report, that Amy had some contagious disease. Curly had made a deal of the sore throat Amy had confessed to.

"And if that's so," Helen said, almost in tears, "poor Ruth will be quarantined for weeks."

"Why, Helen, how will she graduate?" gasped Lluella.

"She won't! She can't!" declared Ruth's chum. "It will be dreadful!"

"I say!" cried Jennie, thoroughly alarmed. "We musn't let her stay there and nurse that young one. Why! what ever would we do if Ruthie Fielding didn't graduate?"

"The class would be without a head," declared Mercy.

"It would be without a heart, at least—and a great, big one overflowing with love and tenderness," cried Nettie Parsons, wiping her eyes.

"I don't want any more breakfast," said Jennie, pushing her plate away. "Don't talk like that, Nettie. You'll get me to crying too. And that always spoils my digestion."

"If Ruth isn't with us when we get our diplomas, I'm sure I don't want any!" exclaimed Mary Cox. And she meant it, too. Mary Cox believed that she owed her brother's life to Ruth Fielding, and although she was not naturally a demonstrative girl, there was nobody at Briarwood Hall who admired the girl of the Red Mill more than Mary.

In fact, the threat of disaster to Ruth's graduation plans cast a pall of gloom over the school. The moving pictures were forgotten; Amy Gregg's part in the destruction of the West Dormitory ceased to be a topic of conversation. Was Ruth Fielding going to be held in quarantine? grew to be a more momentous question than any other.

Ruth, however, was only absent from her accustomed haunts for two days. The second day she remained to attend the patient because Amy begged so hard to have her stay.

In her weakness and pain the sullen, secretive girl had turned instinctively to the one person who had been uniformly gentle and kind to her throughout all her trouble. Nothing that Amy had done or said, had turned Ruth from her; and the barriers of girl's nature and of her evil passions were broken down.

It was not, perhaps, wholly Amy Gregg's fault that her disposition was so warped. She had received bad advice from some aunts, who had likewise set the child a bad example in their treatment of Mr. Gregg's second wife, when he had brought her home to be a mother to Amy.

The poor child suffered so much from the effect of the poison ivy that the other girls, and not alone those of her own grade, "just *had* to be sorry for Amy," as Mary Pease said.

"To think!" said that excitable young girl. "She might even lose her eyesight if she's not careful. My! it must be dreadful to get poisoned with that nasty ivy. I'll be afraid to go into the woods the whole summer."

Of course, it took time for these sentiments to circulate through the school, and for a better feeling for Amy Gregg to come to the surface; but the poor girl was laid up for two weeks in Mrs. Sadoc Smith's best bedroom, and a fortnight is a long time in a girls' boarding school. At least, it sometimes seems so to the pupils.

What helped change the girls' opinion of Amy, too, was the fact that Mrs. Tellingham announced in chapel one morning that Mr. Gregg had sent his check for five hundred dollars toward the rebuilding of the dormitory, the walls of which now were completed, and the roof on.

She spoke, too, of the reason Amy had left her candle burning in her lonely room in the old West Dormitory that fatal evening. "We failed in our duty, both as teachers and fellow-pupils," Mrs. Tellingham said. "I hope that no other girl who enters Briarwood Hall will ever be neglected and left alone as Amy Gregg was, no matter what the new comer's disposition or attitude toward us may be."

To hear the principal take herself to task for lack of foresight and kindness to a new pupil, made a deep impression upon the school at large, and when Amy Gregg appeared on the campus again she was welcomed with gentleness by the other girls. Although Amy Gregg still doubted and shrank from them for some time, before the end of the term she had her chums, and was one of a set whose bright, particular star was her one-time enemy, Mary Pease.

Meanwhile, the older girls—the seniors who were to graduate—had a new problem. The films for "The Heart of a Schoolgirl" were reported almost ready. Mr. Hammond was to release them as soon as he could, in order to bring all the aid to the dormitory fund possible before the end of the semester.

Now the query was, "How is the picture to be advertised?" Merely the ordinary billing in front of the picture playhouses and on the display boards, was not enough. An interest must be stirred of a deeper and broader nature than that which such a casual manner of advertising could be expected to engender.

"How'll we do it?" demanded Jennie, with as much solemnity as it was possible for her rosy, round face to express. "We should invent some catch-phrase to introduce the great film—something as effective as 'Good evening! have you used Higgin's Toothpaste?' or, 'You-must-have-a pound-cake.' You know, something catchy that will stick in people's minds."

"It has taken years and years to make some of those catchy trademarks universal," objected Ruth, seriously. "Our advertising must be done in a hurry."

"Well, we've got to put our best foot forward, somehow," declared Helen. "Everybody must be made to know that the Briarwood girls have a show of their own—a five-reel film that is a corker—"

"Hear! hear!" cried Belle. "Wait till the censor gets hold of *that* word."

"Quite right," agreed Ruth. "Let us be lady-like, though the heavens fall!"

"And still be natural?" chuckled Jennie. "Impossible!"

"Her best foot forward—one's best foot forward." Mary Cox kept repeating Helen's remark while the other girls chattered. Mary had a talent for drawing. "Say!" she suddenly excl- aimed. "I could make a dandy poster with that for a text."

"With what for a text?" somebody asked.

"'Putting One's Best Foot Forward,'" declared Mary Cox, and suddenly seizing charcoal and paper, she sketched the idea quickly—a smartly dressed up-to-date Briarwood girl with her right foot advanced—and that foot, as in a foreshortened photograph—of enormous size.

The poster took with the girls immensely. There was something chic about the figure, and the face, while looking like nobody in particular, was a composite of several of the girls. At least, it was an inspiration on the part of Mary Cox, and when Mrs. Tellingham saw it, she approved.

"We'll just send this 'Big Foot Girl' broadcast," cried Helen, who was proud that her spoken word had been the inspiration for Mary's clever cartoon. "Come on! we'll have it stamped on our stationery, and write to everyone we know bespeaking their best attention when they see the poster in their vicinity."

"And we'll have new postcards made of Briarwood Hall, with Mary's figure printed on the reverse," Sarah Fish said.

They sent a proof of the poster to Mr. Hammond, and to his billing of "The Heart of a Schoolgirl" he immediately added "The Briarwood Girl with Her Best Foot Forward." Locally, during the next few weeks, this poster became immensely popular.

The campaign of advertising did not end with Mary's poster—no, indeed! In every way they could think of the girls of Briarwood Hall spread the tidings of the forthcoming release of the school play.

Lumberton's advertising space was plastered with the Briarwood Girl and with other billing weeks before the film could be seen. As every moving picture theatre in the place clamored for the film, Mr. Hammond had refused to book it with any. The Opera House was engaged for three days and nights, a high price for tickets asked, and it was expected that a goodly sum would be raised for the dormitory right at home.

However, before the picture of "The Heart of a Schoolgirl" came to town, something else happened in the career of Ruth Fielding of the Red Mill which greatly influenced her future.

Alice B. Emerson

CHAPTER XXIV

"SEEING OURSELVES AS OTHERS SEE US"

"I want to tell you girls one thing," said Jennie Stone, solemnly. "If I get through these examinations without having so low a mark that Miss Brokaw sends me down into the primary grade, I promise to be good for—for—well, for the rest of my life—at Briarwood!"

"Of course," Helen said. "Heavy would limit that vow to something easy."

"Perhaps she had the same grave doubt about being able to be good that the little boy felt who was saying his prayers," Belle said. "He prayed: 'Dear God, please make me a good boy—and if You don't at first succeed, try, try again!'"

"But oh! some of the problems *are* so hard," sighed Lluella.

"'The Mournful Sisters' will now give their famous sketch," laughed Ruth, as announcer. "Come, now! altogether, girls!"

"'Knock, knock, knock! the girls are knocking—Bring the hammers all this way!'"

"Never mind, Ruthie Fielding," complained Lluella. "We

don't all of us have the luck you do. All your English made up for you in that scenario—"

"And who is *this* made up, I'd be glad to have somebody tell me?" interposed Jennie. "Oh, girls! tell me. Do you all see the same thing I do?"

The crowd were strolling slowly down the Cedar Walk and the individual the plump girl had spied had just come into view, walking toward them. He was a tall, lean man, "as narrow as a happy thought," Jennie muttered, and dressed in a peculiar manner.

Few visitors came to Briarwood save parents or friends of the girls. This man did not even look like a pedler. At least, he carried no sample case, and he was not walking from the direction of Lumberton.

His black suit was very dusty and his yellow shoes proved by the dust they bore, too, that he had walked a long way.

"He wears a rolling collar and a flowing tie," muttered the irrepressible Jennie. "Goodness! it almost makes me seasick to look at them. *What* can he be? A chaplain in the navy? An actor?"

"Actor is right," thought Ruth, as the man strutted up the walk.

The girls, who were attending Ruth and Ann and Amy Gregg a part of the way to Mrs. Sadoc Smith's, gave the strange man plenty of room on the gravel walk, but when he came near them he stopped and stared. And he stared at Ruth.

"Pardon me, young lady," he said, in a full, sonorous tone. "Are you Miss Fielding?"

The other girls drifted away and left Ruth to face the odd looking person.

"I am Ruth Fielding," Ruth said, much puzzled.

"Ah! you do not know me?" queried the man.

"No, sir."

"My card!" said the man, with a flourish.

Jennie whispered to the others: "Look at him! He draws and presents that card as though it were a sword at his enemy's throat! I hope he won't impale her upon it."

Ruth, much bewildered, and not a little troubled, accepted the card. On it was printed:

AMASA FARRINGTON
Criterion Films

"Goodness!" thought Ruth. "More moving picture people?"

"I had the happiness," stated Mr. Farrington, "of being present when the censors saw the first run of your eminently successful picture, 'The Heart of a Schoolgirl,' Miss Fielding, and through a mutual friend I learned where you were to be found. I may say that from your appearance on the screen I was enabled to recognize you just now."

Ruth said nothing, but waited for him to explain. There really did not seem to be anything she could say.

"I see in that film, Miss Fielding," pursued Mr. Farrington, "the promise of better work—in time, of course, in time. You are young yet. I believe you attend this boarding school?"

"Yes," said Ruth, simply.

"From the maturity of your treatment of the scenario I fancied you might be a teacher here at Briarwood," pursued the man, smirking. "But I find you a young person— extremely young, if I may be allowed the observation, to have written a scenario of the character of 'The Heart of a Schoolgirl.'"

"I wrote it," said Ruth, for she thought the remark was a question. "I had written one before."

"Yes, yes, yes!" exclaimed Mr. Farrington. "So I understand. In fact, I have seen your 'Curiosity.' A very ingeniously thought out reel. And well acted by the Alectrion Company. Rather good acting, indeed, for *them*."

"I have not seen it myself," Ruth said, not knowing what the man wanted or how she ought to speak to him. "Did you wish to talk to me on any matter of importance?"

"I may say, Yes, very important—to yourself, Miss Fielding," he said, with a wide smile. "This is a most important matter. It affects your entire career as—I may say—one of our most ingenious young writers for the screen."

Ruth stared at him in amazement. Just because she had written two moving picture scenarios she was quite sure that she was neither famous nor a genius. Mr. Amasa Farrington's enthusiasm was more amazing than his appearance.

"I am sure I do not understand you," Ruth confessed. "Is it something that you would better talk to Mrs. Tellingham about? I will introduce you to her—"

"No, no!" said Mr. Farrington, waving a black-gloved hand

with the gesture *Hamlet* might have used in waving to his father's ghost. "The lady preceptress of your school has naught to do with this matter. It is personal with you."

"But what *is* it?" queried Ruth, rather exasperated now.

"Be not hasty—be not hasty, I beg," said Amasa Farrington. "I know I may surprise you. I, too, was unknown at one time, and never expected to be anything more than a traveling Indian Bitters pedler. My latent talent was developed and fostered by a kindly soul, and I come to you now, Miss Fielding, in the remembrance of my own youth and inexperience—"

"For mercy's sake!" gasped Ruth, finally. "What do you wish? I am not in need of any Indian Bitters."

"You mistake me—you mistake me," said the man, stiffly. "Amasa Farrington has long since graduated from the ranks of such sordid toilers. See my card."

"I *do* see your card," the impatient Ruth said, again glancing at the bit of pasteboard. "I see that you represent something called the 'Criterion Films.' What are they?"

"Ah! now you ask a pointed question, young lady," declared Mr. Farrington. "Rather you should ask, 'What will they be?' They will be the most widely advertised films ever released for the entertainment of the public. They will be written by the most famous writers of scenarios. They will be produced by the greatest directors in the business. They will be acted by our foremost Thespians."

"I—I hope you will be successful, Mr. Farrington," said Ruth, faintly, not knowing what else to say.

"We shall be—we must be—I may say that we have *got* to be!" ejaculated the ex-Indian Bitters pedler. "And I come to you, Miss Fielding, for your co-operation."

"Mine?" gasped Ruth.

"Yes, Miss Fielding. You are a coming writer of scenarios of a high character. We geniuses must help each other—we must keep together and refuse to further the ends of the sordid producers who would bleed us of our best work."

This was rather wild talk, and Ruth did not understand it. She said, frankly:

"Just what do you mean, Mr. Farrington? What do you want me to do?"

"Ah! Practical! I like to see you so," said the man, with a flourish, drawing forth a document of several typewritten pages. "I want you to read and sign this, Miss Fielding. It is a contract with the Criterion Films—a most liberal contract, I might say—in which you bind yourself to turn over to us your scenarios for a term of years, we, meanwhile, agreeing to push your work and make you known to the public."

"Oh, dear me!" gasped Ruth. "I'm not sure I want to be so publicly known."

"Nonsense!" cried the man, in amazement. "Why! in publicity is the breath of life. Without it, we faint—we die—we, worse—we *vegetate*!"

"I—I guess I don't mind vegetating—a—a little," stammered Ruth, weakly.

At that moment Mary Pease came racing down the walk. She

Alice B. Emerson

waved a letter in her hand and was calling Ruth's name.

"Oh, Ruthie Fielding!" she called, when she saw Ruth with the man. "Here's a letter Mrs. Tellingham forgot to give you. She says it came enclosed in one from Mr. Hammond to her."

The excited girl stopped by Ruth, handed her the letter, and stared frankly at Mr. Amasa Farrington. That person's face began to redden as Ruth idly opened the unsealed missive.

Again a green slip fell out. Mary darted toward it and picked it up. She read the check loudly—excitedly—almost in a shriek!

"Goodness, gracious me, Ruthie Fielding! Is Mr. Hammond giving you this money—*all* this money—for your very own?"

But Ruth did not reply. She was scanning the letter from the president of the Alectrion Film Corporation. Mr. Farrington was plainly nervous.

"Come, Miss Fielding, I am waiting for your answer," he said stiffly. "If you join the Criterion Films, your success is assured. You are famous from the start—"

Ruth was just reading a clause in Mr. Hammond's kind and friendly letter:

"Don't let your head be turned by success, little girl. And I don't think it will be. You have succeeded in inventing two very original scenarios. We will hope you can do better work in time. But don't force yourself. Above all have nothing to do with agents of film people who may want you to write something that they may rush into the market for the benefit of the advertising your school play will give you."

"No, Mr. Farrington," said Ruth, kindly. "I do not want to join your forces. I am not even sure that I shall ever be able to write another scenario. Circumstances seemed really to force me to write 'The Heart of a Schoolgirl.' I am glad you think well of it. Good afternoon."

"Can you beat her?" demanded Jennie, a minute later, when the long-legged Mr. Farrington had strutted angrily away. "Ruthie is as calm as a summer lake. She can turn an offer of fame and fortune down with the greatest ease. Let's see that check, you miserable infant," she went on, grabbing the slip of paper out of Mary's hand. "Oh, girls, it's really so!"

Ruth was reading another paragraph in Mr. Hammond's letter. He said:

"The check enclosed is for you, yourself. It has nothing to do with the profits of the films we now release. It is a bribe. I want to see whatever scenarios you may write during the next two years. I want to see them first. That is all. We do not need a contract, but if you keep the check I shall know that I am to have first choice of anything you may write in this line."

The check went into Ruth's bank account.

That very week "The Heart of a Schoolgirl" was to be shown at the local Opera House. Mrs. Tellingham gave a half holiday and engaged enough stages besides Noah's old Ark, to take all the girls to the play. They went to the matinee, and the center of enthusiasm was in the seats in the body of the house reserved for the Briarwood girls.

Alice B. Emerson

The house was well filled at this first showing of the picture in Lumberton, and more than the girls themselves were enthusiastic over it. To Ruth's surprise the manager of the house showed "Curiosity" first, and when she saw her name emblazoned under the title of the one-reel film, Ruth Fielding had a distinct shock.

It was a joyful feeling that shook her, however. As never before she realized that she had really accomplished something in the world. She had earned money with her brains! And she had written something really worth while, too.

When the five-reel drama came on, she was as much absorbed in the story as though she had not written it and acted in it. It gave her a strange feeling indeed when she saw herself come on to the screen, and knew just what she was saying in the picture by the movement of her lips—whether she remembered the words spoken when the film was made or not.

Everything went off smoothly. The girls cheered the picture to the echo, and at the end went marching out, shouting:

"S.B.—Ah-h-h!
S.B.—Ah-h-h!
Sound our battle-cry
Near and far!
S.B.—All!
Briarwood Hall!
Sweetbriars,
do or die—
This be our battle-cry—
Briarwood Hall!
That's all!"

CHAPTER XXV

AUNT ALVIRAH AT BRIARWOOD HALL

Mr. Cameron, Helen's father, and Mrs. Murchiston, who had acted as governess for the twins until they were old enough to go to boarding school, were motoring to Briarwood Hall for the graduation exercises. They proposed to pick Tom up at Seven Oaks Military Academy, for he would spend another year at that school, not graduating until the following June.

They also had another guest in the big automobile who took up a deal of the attention of the drygoods merchant and Mrs. Murchiston. A two-days' trip was made of it, the party staying at a hotel for the night. Aunt Alvirah was going farther from the Red Mill and the town of Cheslow than she had ever been in her life before.

First she said she could not possibly do it! What ever would Jabez do without her? And he would not hear to it, anyway. And then—there was "her back and her bones."

"Best place for old folks like me is in the chimbly corner," declared Aunt Alvirah. "Much as I would love to see my pretty graduate with all them other gals, I don't see how I can do it. It's like uprooting a tree that's growed all its life in one

Alice B. Emerson

spot. I'm deep-rooted at the Red Mill."

But Mr. Cameron knew it was the wish of the old woman's heart to see "her pretty" graduate from Briarwood Hall. It had been Aunt Alvirah's word that had made possible Ruth's first going to school with Helen Cameron. It was she who had urged Mr. Jabez Potter on, term after term, to give the girl the education she so craved.

Indeed, Aunt Alvirah had been the good angel of Ruth's existence at the Red Mill. Nobody in the world had so deep an interest in the young girl as the little old woman who hobbled around the Red Mill kitchen.

Therefore Mr. Cameron was determined that she should go to Briarwood. He fairly shamed Mr. Potter into hiring a woman to come in to do for Ben and himself while Aunt Alvirah was gone.

"You ought to shut up your mill altogether and go yourself, Potter," declared Mr. Cameron. "Think what your girl has done. I'm proud of my daughter. You should be doubly proud of your niece."

"Well, who says I'm not?" snarled Jabez Potter. "But I can't afford to leave my work to run about to such didoes."

"You'll be sorry some day," suggested Mr. Cameron. "But, at any rate, Aunt Alvirah shall go."

And the trip was one of wonder to Aunt Alvirah Boggs. First she was alarmed, for she confessed to a fear of automobiles. But when she felt the huge machine which carried them so swiftly over the roads running so smoothly, Aunt Alvirah became a convert to the new method of locomotion.

At the hotel where they halted for the night, there were more wonders. Aunt Alvirah's knowledge of modern conveniences was from reading only. She had never before been nearer to a telephone than to look up at the wires that were strung from post to post before the Red Mill. Modern plumbing, an elevator, heating by steam, and many other improvements, were like a sealed book to her.

She disliked to be waited upon and whispered to Mrs. Murchiston:

"That air black man a-standin' behind my chair at dinner sort o' makes me narvous. I'm expectin' of him to grab my plate away before I'm done eatin'."

The day set for the graduation exercises at Briarwood Hall was as lovely a June day as was ever seen. The Cameron automobile rolled into the grounds and was parked with several dozen machines, just as the girls were marching into chapel. The fresh young voices chanting "One Wide River to Cross" floated across to the ears of the party from the Red Mill, and Aunt Alvirah began to hum the song in her cracked, sweet treble.

The automobile party followed the smaller girls along the wide walk of the campus. There was the new West Dormitory, quite completed on the outside, and sufficiently so inside for the seniors to occupy rooms. Not the old quartettes and duos of times past; but very beautiful rooms nevertheless, in which they could later entertain their friends who had come to the graduation exercises.

The organist began to play softly on the great organ in the chapel, and played until every girl was seated—the graduating class upon the platform. Then the school orchestra played and Helen—very pretty in white with cherry ribbons

—stood forth with her violin and played a solo.

Mrs. Tellingham welcomed the visitors in a short speech. Then there was a little silence before the strains of an old, old song quivered through the big chapel. Helen was playing again, with the soft tones of the organ as a background. And, in a moment Ruth stood up, stepped forward, and began to sing.

The Cheslow party had all heard her before. She was almost always singing about the old Red Mill when she was at home. But into this ballad she seemed to put more feeling than ever before. The tears ran down Aunt Alvirah's withered cheeks. Ruth did not know the dear old woman was present, for it was to be a surprise to her; but she might have been singing just for Aunt Alvirah alone.

"This pays me for coming, Miz' Murchiston, if nothin' else would," whispered Aunt Alvirah. "I can see my pretty often and often, I hope. But I'll never hear her sing again like this."

The exercises went smoothly. A learned man made a helpful speech. Then, while there was more music, a curtain fell between the graduating class and the audience.

When it rose again the girls were grouped about a light throne, trimmed with flowers, on which sat the girl who had proved herself to be the best scholar of them all—the lame girl, Mercy Curtis. She was flushed, she was excited and, if never before, Mercy Curtis looked actually pretty.

Laughing and singing, her mates rolled the throne down to the edge of the platform, and there, still sitting in her pretty, flowing white robes, Mercy gave them the valedictory oration. It was Ruth's idea, filched from the transformation scene in her moving picture scenario.

Afterward the other girls had their turns. Ruth's own paper upon "The Force of Character" and Jennie's funny "History of a Bunch of Briers" received the most applause.

Mrs. Tellingham came last. As was her custom she spoke briefly of the work of the past year and her hopes for the next one; but mainly she lingered upon the story of the rebuilding of the West Dormitory and the loyalty the girls had shown in making the new building a possibility.

There was a debt upon it yet; but the royalties from the picture play were coming in most satisfactorily. The preceptress urged all her guests to do what they could to advertise the film of "The Heart of a Schoolgirl" in their home towns, and especially urged them to see it.

"You will be well repaid. Not alone because it is a true picture of our boarding school life, but because the writer of the scenario has produced a good and helpful story, and Mr. Hammond has put it on the screen with taste and judgment."

These were Mrs. Tellingham's words, and they made Ruth Fielding very proud.

The diplomas were given out after a touching address by the local clergyman. The girls received the parchments with happy hearts. Their faces shone and their eyes were bright.

The graduating class held a sort of reception on the platform; but after a time Helen urged Ruth away from the crowd. "Come on!" she said. "Let's go up into the new-old-room. We'll not have many chances of being in it now."

"That's right. Only to-night," sighed Ruth. "Away to-morrow for the Red Mill. And next week we start for Dixie. I wonder if we shall have a good time, Helen. Do you think we ought to have promised Nettie and her aunt that we would come?"

"Surely! Why, we'll have a dandy time," declared Helen, "just us girls alone."

This belief proved true in the end, as may be learned in the next volume of this series, to be entitled "Ruth Fielding Down in Dixie; Or, Great Days in the Land of Cotton."

"I didn't see your father or Tom or Mrs. Murchiston," Ruth said, as she and Helen walked across the campus.

"They are here, just the same," said Helen, laughing.

"Where?"

"I shouldn't be surprised if we found them up in our old quartette. Ann is with her Uncle Bill Hicks, and Mercy is with her father and mother. We shall have the room to ourselves. We'll get out my new tea set and give them tea. Come on!"

Helen raced up the stairs, opened the door of the big room, and then got behind it so that Ruth, coming hurriedly in, should first see the little, quivering, eager figure which had risen out of the low chair by the window.

"My pretty! my pretty!" gasped Aunt Alvirah. "I seen you graduate, and I heard you sing, and I listened to your fine readin'. But, oh, my pretty, how hungry my arms are for ye!"

She hobbled across the floor to meet Ruth and, for once, forgot her usually intoned complaint: "Oh, my back! and oh, my bones!" Ruth caught her in her strong young arms. Helen slipped out and joined her family in the hall.

In a little while Tom thundered on the door, and shouted: "Hey! we're dying for that cup of tea Helen promised us, Ruthie Fielding. Aren't you ever going to let us in?"

Ruth's smiling face immediately appeared. Her eyes were still wet and her lips trembled as she said:

"Come in, all of you, do! We are sure to have a nice cup of tea. Aunt Alvirah is making it herself."

THE END

Alice B. Emerson

Choose from Thousands of 1stWorldLibrary Classics By

A. M. Barnard
Ada Leverson
Adolphus William Ward
Aesop
Agatha Christie
Alexander Aaronsohn
Alexander Kielland
Alexandre Dumas
Alfred Gatty
Alfred Ollivant
Alice Duer Miller
Alice Turner Curtis
Alice Dunbar
Allen Chapman
Alleyne Ireland
Ambrose Bierce
Amelia E. Barr
Amory H. Bradford
Andrew Lang
Andrew McFarland Davis
Andy Adams
Angela Brazil
Anna Alice Chapin
Anna Sewell
Annie Besant
Annie Hamilton Donnell
Annie Payson Call
Annie Roe Carr
Annonaymous
Anton Chekhov
Archibald Lee Fletcher
Arnold Bennett
Arthur C. Benson
Arthur Conan Doyle
Arthur M. Winfield
Arthur Ransome
Arthur Schnitzler
Arthur Train
Atticus
B.H. Baden-Powell
B. M. Bower
B. C. Chatterjee
Baroness Emmuska Orczy
Baroness Orczy
Basil King
Bayard Taylor
Ben Macomber
Bertha Muzzy Bower
Bjornstjerne Bjornson

Booth Tarkington
Boyd Cable
Bram Stoker
C. Collodi
C. E. Orr
C. M. Ingleby
Carolyn Wells
Catherine Parr Traill
Charles A. Eastman
Charles Amory Beach
Charles Dickens
Charles Dudley Warner
Charles Farrar Browne
Charles Ives
Charles Kingsley
Charles Klein
Charles Hanson Towne
Charles Lathrop Pack
Charles Romyn Dake
Charles Whibley
Charles Willing Beale
Charlotte M. Braeme
Charlotte M. Yonge
Charlotte Perkins Stetson
Clair W. Hayes
Clarence Day Jr.
Clarence E. Mulford
Clemence Housman
Confucius
Coningsby Dawson
Cornelis DeWitt Wilcox
Cyril Burleigh
D. H. Lawrence
Daniel Defoe
David Garnett
Dinah Craik
Don Carlos Janes
Donald Keyhoe
Dorothy Kilner
Dougan Clark
Douglas Fairbanks
E. Nesbit
E. P. Roe
E. Phillips Oppenheim
E. S. Brooks
Earl Barnes
Edgar Rice Burroughs
Edith Van Dyne
Edith Wharton

Edward Everett Hale
Edward J. O'Biren
Edward S. Ellis
Edwin L. Arnold
Eleanor Atkins
Eleanor Hallowell Abbott
Eliot Gregory
Elizabeth Gaskell
Elizabeth McCracken
Elizabeth Von Arnim
Ellem Key
Emerson Hough
Emilie F. Carlen
Emily Bronte
Emily Dickinson
Enid Bagnold
Enilor Macartney Lane
Erasmus W. Jones
Ernie Howard Pie
Ethel May Dell
Ethel Turner
Ethel Watts Mumford
Eugene Sue
Eugenie Foa
Eugene Wood
Eustace Hale Ball
Evelyn Everett-green
Everard Cotes
F. H. Cheley
F. J. Cross
F. Marion Crawford
Fannie E. Newberry
Federick Austin Ogg
Ferdinand Ossendowski
Fergus Hume
Florence A. Kilpatrick
Fremont B. Deering
Francis Bacon
Francis Darwin
Frances Hodgson Burnett
Frances Parkinson Keyes
Frank Gee Patchin
Frank Harris
Frank Jewett Mather
Frank L. Packard
Frank V. Webster
Frederic Stewart Isham
Frederick Trevor Hill
Frederick Winslow Taylor

Friedrich Kerst
Friedrich Nietzsche
Fyodor Dostoyevsky
G.A. Henty
G.K. Chesterton
Gabrielle E. Jackson
Garrett P. Serviss
Gaston Leroux
George A. Warren
George Ade
Geroge Bernard Shaw
George Cary Eggleston
George Durston
George Ebers
George Eliot
George Gissing
George MacDonald
George Meredith
George Orwell
George Sylvester Viereck
George Tucker
George W. Cable
George Wharton James
Gertrude Atherton
Gordon Casserly
Grace E. King
Grace Gallatin
Grace Greenwood
Grant Allen
Guillermo A. Sherwell
Gulielma Zollinger
Gustav Flaubert
H. A. Cody
H. B. Irving
H.C. Bailey
H. G. Wells
H. H. Munro
H. Irving Hancock
H. R. Naylor
H. Rider Haggard
H. W. C. Davis
Haldeman Julius
Hall Caine
Hamilton Wright Mabie
Hans Christian Andersen
Harold Avery
Harold McGrath
Harriet Beecher Stowe
Harry Castlemon
Harry Coghill
Harry Houidini

Hayden Carruth
Helent Hunt Jackson
Helen Nicolay
Hendrik Conscience
Hendy David Thoreau
Henri Barbusse
Henrik Ibsen
Henry Adams
Henry Ford
Henry Frost
Henry James
Henry Jones Ford
Henry Seton Merriman
Henry W Longfellow
Herbert A. Giles
Herbert Carter
Herbert N. Casson
Herman Hesse
Hildegard G. Frey
Homer
Honore De Balzac
Horace B. Day
Horace Walpole
Horatio Alger Jr.
Howard Pyle
Howard R. Garis
Hugh Lofting
Hugh Walpole
Humphry Ward
Ian Maclaren
Inez Haynes Gillmore
Irving Bacheller
Isabel Cecilia Williams
Isabel Hornibrook
Israel Abrahams
Ivan Turgenev
J.G.Austin
J. Henri Fabre
J. M. Barrie
J. M. Walsh
J. Macdonald Oxley
J. R. Miller
J. S. Fletcher
J. S. Knowles
J. Storer Clouston
J. W. Duffield
Jack London
Jacob Abbott
James Allen
James Andrews
James Baldwin

James Branch Cabell
James DeMille
James Joyce
James Lane Allen
James Lane Allen
James Oliver Curwood
James Oppenheim
James Otis
James R. Driscoll
Jane Abbott
Jane Austen
Jane L. Stewart
Janet Aldridge
Jens Peter Jacobsen
Jerome K. Jerome
Jessie Graham Flower
John Buchan
John Burroughs
John Cournos
John F. Kennedy
John Gay
John Glasworthy
John Habberton
John Joy Bell
John Kendrick Bangs
John Milton
John Philip Sousa
John Taintor Foote
Jonas Lauritz Idemil Lie
Jonathan Swift
Joseph A. Altsheler
Joseph Carey
Joseph Conrad
Joseph E. Badger Jr
Joseph Hergesheimer
Joseph Jacobs
Jules Vernes
Julian Hawthrone
Julie A Lippmann
Justin Huntly McCarthy
Kakuzo Okakura
Karle Wilson Baker
Kate Chopin
Kenneth Grahame
Kenneth McGaffey
Kate Langley Bosher
Kate Langley Bosher
Katherine Cecil Thurston
Katherine Stokes
L. A. Abbot
L. T. Meade

L. Frank Baum
Latta Griswold
Laura Dent Crane
Laura Lee Hope
Laurence Housman
Lawrence Beasley
Leo Tolstoy
Leonid Andreyev
Lewis Carroll
Lewis Sperry Chafer
Lilian Bell
Lloyd Osbourne
Louis Hughes
Louis Joseph Vance
Louis Tracy
Louisa May Alcott
Lucy Fitch Perkins
Lucy Maud Montgomery
Luther Benson
Lydia Miller Middleton
Lyndon Orr
M. Corvus
M. H. Adams
Margaret E. Sangster
Margret Howth
Margaret Vandercook
Margaret W. Hungerford
Margret Penrose
Maria Edgeworth
Maria Thompson Daviess
Mariano Azuela
Marion Polk Angellotti
Mark Overton
Mark Twain
Mary Austin
Mary Catherine Crowley
Mary Cole
Mary Hastings Bradley
Mary Roberts Rinehart
Mary Rowlandson
M. Wollstonecraft Shelley
Maud Lindsay
Max Beerbohm
Myra Kelly
Nathaniel Hawthrone
Nicolo Machiavelli
O. F. Walton
Oscar Wilde

Owen Johnson
P.G. Wodehouse
Paul and Mabel Thorne
Paul G. Tomlinson
Paul Severing
Percy Brebner
Percy Keese Fitzhugh
Peter B. Kyne
Plato
Quincy Allen
R. Derby Holmes
R. L. Stevenson
R. S. Ball
Rabindranath Tagore
Rahul Alvares
Ralph Bonehill
Ralph Henry Barbour
Ralph Victor
Ralph Waldo Emmerson
Rene Descartes
Ray Cummings
Rex Beach
Rex E. Beach
Richard Harding Davis
Richard Jefferies
Richard Le Gallienne
Robert Barr
Robert Frost
Robert Gordon Anderson
Robert L. Drake
Robert Lansing
Robert Lynd
Robert Michael Ballantyne
Robert W. Chambers
Rosa Nouchette Carey
Rudyard Kipling
Saint Augustine
Samuel B. Allison
Samuel Hopkins Adams
Sarah Bernhardt
Sarah C. Hallowell
Selma Lagerlof
Sherwood Anderson
Sigmund Freud
Standish O'Grady
Stanley Weyman
Stella Benson
Stella M. Francis

Stephen Crane
Stewart Edward White
Stijn Streuvels
Swami Abhedananda
Swami Parmananda
T. S. Ackland
T. S. Arthur
The Princess Der Ling
Thomas A. Janvier
Thomas A Kempis
Thomas Anderton
Thomas Bailey Aldrich
Thomas Bulfinch
Thomas De Quincey
Thomas Dixon
Thomas H. Huxley
Thomas Hardy
Thomas More
Thornton W. Burgess
U. S. Grant
Upton Sinclair
Valentine Williams
Various Authors
Vaughan Kester
Victor Appleton
Victor G. Durham
Victoria Cross
Virginia Woolf
Wadsworth Camp
Walter Camp
Walter Scott
Washington Irving
Wilbur Lawton
Wilkie Collins
Willa Cather
Willard F. Baker
William Dean Howells
William le Queux
W. Makepeace Thackeray
William W. Walter
William Shakespeare
Winston Churchill
Yei Theodora Ozaki
Yogi Ramacharaka
Young E. Allison
Zane Grey

www.ingramcontent.com/pod-product-compliance
Lightning Source LLC
Chambersburg PA
CBHW050530260626
47157CB00004B/1546